D0832215

The Virtues of Poetry

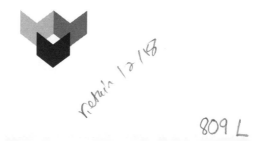

Also by James Longenbach

Poetry

The Iron Key
Draft of a Letter
Fleet River
Threshold

Prose

The Art of the Poetic Line
The Resistance to Poetry
Modern Poetry after Modernism
Wallace Stevens
Stone Cottage

The Virtues of Poetry

James Longenbach

GRAYWOLF PRESS

"Fan-Piece, For Her Imperial Lord" by Ezra Pound, from *Personae*, copyright © 1926 by Ezra Pound. Reprinted by permission of New Directions Publishing Corp.

This publication is made possible, in part, by the voters of Minnesota through a Minnesota State Arts Board Operating Support grant, thanks to a legislative appropriation from the arts and cultural heritage fund, and through a grant from the National Endowment for the Arts. Significant support has also been provided by Target, the McKnight Foundation, Amazon.com, and other generous contributions from foundations, corporations, and individuals. To these organizations and individuals we offer our heartfelt thanks.

Published by Graywolf Press
250 Third Avenue North, Suite 600
Minneapolis, Minnesota 55401

www.graywolfpress.org

Published in the United States of America

ISBN 978-1-55597-637-8

2 4 6 8 9 7 5 3 1
First Graywolf Printing, 2013

Library of Congress Control Number: 2012953981

Cover design: Kimberly Glyder Design

Cover photos: Walker and Walker, The Image Bank, Getty Images (top) / Copyright Karen Ilagen, Flickr, Getty Images (bottom)

The source of poetry is always a mystery, an inspiration, a charged perplexity in the face of the irrational—unknown territory. But the act of poetry—if one may make a distinction here, separating the flame from the fuel—is an absolute determination to see clearly, to reduce to reason, to know.

—Cesare Pavese

Contents

Preface   ix

The Various Light   3
Best Thought   17
Less Than Everything   27
Writing Badly   41
The Door Ajar   55
Infinitude   65
A Fine Excess   77
Correct Catastrophe   91
The Visible Core   101
The Opposite of Risk   113
Poetry Thinking   125
All Changed   141

Acknowledgments   159
Bibliography   161
Index   165

Preface

The best poems ever written constitute our future. They re-fine our notions of excellence by continuing to elude them. Any utterance affords us an opportunity to think about diction, rhythm, structure, and tone, but by asking to be heard as well as understood, poems intensify our relationship with the medium, the medium we harness every day. No great poem ever stood in the way of the future, foreclosing imaginative possibilities by asking us to endorse a narrow vision of our past or a sectarian arrangement of our contemporaries.

But over the past fifty years, accomplishment in our poetry has been signaled most often by manner—as if it were the job of artists not to engage the most potent aspects of Dickinson or Eliot but to sequester themselves in one or another schoolroom, buoyed by the camaraderie with other students sitting obedi-ently, if stylishly, in rows. Schoolroom for formalists, school-room for experimentalists—the degeneration of these terms, hijacked by the renegade engines of taste, would portend the degeneration of the medium, except that while fifty years is a long time in the life of an artist, it is in the history of art noth-ing, the blink of an eye.

This is why the previous fifty years of poetry almost always seem mannered; they seemed so to Yeats a hundred years ago, they seemed so to Keats a hundred years before that. In the short run, the schoolrooms are driven by a mode of writing that can be learned from like-minded contemporaries, releasing poets from the work of learning from inimitable predecessors. But in the long run, Keats did not become Keats by hanging out with Leigh Hunt; he became Keats by spending long, rich hours with Shakespeare and Milton, poets whose virtues he dissected word by word.

This book proposes some of the virtues to which the next poem might aspire: boldness, change, compression, dilation, doubt, excess, inevitability, intimacy, otherness, particularity, restraint, shyness, surprise, and worldliness. The word *virtue* came to English from Latin, via Old French, and while it has acquired a moral valence, the word in its earliest uses gestured toward a magical or transcendental power, a power that might be embodied by any particular substance or act. With vices I am not concerned. Unlike the short-term history of taste, which is fueled by reprimand or correction, the history of art moves from achievement to achievement. Contemporary embodiments of poetry's virtues abound, and only our devotion to a long history of excellence allows us to recognize them.

Certainly there are more virtues than the ones I emphasize, nearly as many as there are poems. So while any of the book's chapters may be read on its own, the chapters are designed to be read in sequence, every poem both challenging and consolidating the embodiments of excellence surrounding it. Sometimes the chapters address each other explicitly, either by opposition (boldness and shyness) or by partially overlapping (boldness and excess). Implicitly the chapters address themselves. The same poet may embody virtues that initially seem unrelated (Shakespeare representing both dilation and surprise) or opposed (Yeats representing both change and inevitability), suggesting that our notions of excellence are not as stable as one might have imagined, also that the poets are themselves more various than any set of virtues may allow. How do we describe the allure of wild excess when we are confronted with the irresistible seduction of restraint? Why does the power of a great poem feel simultaneously unpredictable and assured?

No virtue may be assumed, except inasmuch as it is evinced in a particular way by a particular poem: my interest lies not in abstract notions of excellence but in the ways in which such notions are enacted in language. As Cesare Pavese says in my epigraph, the art of poetry is produced by an absolute determination to see clearly, to reduce to reason; even the thrill of disorder is produced in art by exquisitely crafted means. But as Pavese also says, the source of poetry is an irrational mystery, never to be reasoned, and I also spend some time examining, usually through letters, the lives that these poets have transmuted so painstakingly.

The poets I discuss are hardly unfamiliar; besides the ones I've mentioned so far, I'll also be talking about Donne, Blake, Whitman, Pound, Bishop, and Ashbery, among others. Some poets will be treated at length, and some will need to be discussed more quickly. But the relationships between the poems are as important to me as the poems themselves. Openness is everywhere assumed. That the poets are familiar is a mark not only of virtues we might take for granted but also of a future we might sidestep or dismiss, mistaking it for the past.

The Virtues of Poetry

The Various Light

Celebrating the painter Elstir, the narrator of *In Search of Lost Time* suggests that for the great artist, the work of painting and the act of being alive are indistinguishable. "Certain bodies, certain callings, certain rhythms" may confirm our ideals so inevitably, says Proust, that "merely by copying the movement of a shoulder, the tension of a neck, we can achieve a masterpiece." The implication here is that art is not the product of the will. More than lack of ambition, it is the inability to surrender to our inevitable callings and rhythms that keeps us from fulfilling our promise.

The word *surrender* makes this achievement sound easy, as if the victory of each day were to wake up looking exactly like yourself. But even if we all possess certain rhythms, certain callings, not everyone is able to sustain the simple act of recognizing them. The surrender of the will is itself impossible merely to will, and we may struggle with the act of surrender more deeply than we struggle with the act of rebellion. "Now I may wither into the truth," said W. B. Yeats of this process of recognizing oneself, and the word *wither* seems just right, for the discovery does not feel like a blossoming. Nor does it happen only once, like an inoculation. Proust's Elstir does not inhabit his inevitable self truly until he has achieved great age.

Writers have withered into worldliness and excess; writers have withered into shyness and restraint. Why do the latter

3

virtues so often receive bad press, even from artists who embrace them? In my own experience, plainness can be difficult to separate from dullness, restraint from lack of vision or adequate technique; a young writer may embrace the glamour of excess in order to avoid parsing these discriminations. What's more, the association of artistic achievement with heroic willfulness is endemic, and it is clung to in twenty-first-century America with a fierceness empowered by its fragility: American artists are called great when they are at the frontier, taking the risk, disdaining the status quo, but also landing the movie deal. What happens to the poet who is destined to wither into restraint, the poet whose deepest inclination is to associate risk with submission?

Listen to "The Fish," a poem written by Yeats in the final years of the nineteenth century.

> Although you hide in the ebb and flow
> Of the pale tide when the moon has set,
> The people of coming days will know
> About the casting out of my net,
> And how you have leaped times out of mind
> Over the little silver cords,
> And think that you were hard and unkind,
> And blame you with many bitter words.

That's one sentence made of sixty words. The sixty words contain seventy-one syllables, some of which receive more stress than others, and like every poet who has ever worked with the English language, writing either formal or free verse, Yeats wants us to hear the relationship of the stressed and unstressed syllables in a particular way; that is, he wants to add an unnatural pattern to the way we naturally pronounce the words. Yeats's pattern rests on his decision to have every line of "The Fish" contain four stressed syllables.

> Although you **hide** in the **ebb** and **flow**

But having noticed the consistency of these tetrameter lines, we notice that the consistency exists in tension with an inconsistency. Often only one unstressed syllable precedes a stressed syllable: "Although you **hide**." This is the iambic rhythm familiar to us from so many English poems, but not one line in Yeats's poem is perfectly iambic. Sometimes two unstressed syllables intervene, making an anapestic rhythm: "in the **ebb**." In the third line, the second metrical foot is anapestic ("-ple of **com**"), and in the fourth line, the fourth is anapestic ("of my **net**"). In the second line, the first and third feet are anapests ("Of the **pale**"—"when the **moon**"), and the line is made even wilder by the lack of an unstressed syllable between "pale" and "tide."

> Of the **pale tide** when the **moon** has **set**

Why do these variations matter? One of the great advantages of the English language, as a medium for poetry, is its multiplicity of roots: we are used to hearing our original Anglo-Saxon words nestled against imported French or Latinate words in our poetry. Shakespeare: "seas incarnadine." Blake: "invisible worm." If we find this effect in English translations of Baudelaire or Dante we are hearing something that poems written in French or Italian cannot easily do, since those languages are derived more primarily from Latin alone. But while it's difficult to write English poetry without taking advantage of contrasting roots, this is exactly what Yeats does in "The Fish." The fact that the poem contains sixty words but only seventy-one syllables means that Yeats employs shockingly few multi-syllabic words. Almost every word in the poem is derived from the language's Germanic base (*ebb, flow, tide, moon, set*), and this restraint drives the poem's rhythmic sophistication. Without the subtle variation of the metrical pattern through which the poem's single sentence moves, the poem's almost unrelievedly monosyllabic diction would fall flat.

Yeats was a great Victorian poet who happened to live long enough to become a great modern poet, so we tend not to think of his early verse as an achievement in its own right. But when Ezra Pound looked back over the history of modern poetry in *The Pisan Cantos*, remarking that "to break the pentameter, that was the first heave," he was thinking of the rhythmic delicacy of the early Yeats. Notoriously, Yeats changed, but I hear that delicacy in middle-period Yeats.

> The trees are in their autumn beauty,
> The woodland paths are dry,
> Under the October twilight the water
> Mirrors a still sky;
> Upon the brimming water among the stones
> Are nine-and-fifty swans.

And I hear it in later Yeats as well.

> Under my window-ledge the waters race,
> Otters below and moor-hens on the top,
> Run for a mile undimmed in Heaven's face
> Then darkening through 'dark' Raftery's 'cellar' drop,
> Run underground, rise in a rocky place
> In Coole demesne, and there to finish up
> Spread to a lake and drop into a hole.
> What's water but the generated soul?

From the beginning until the end of his career Yeats delighted in stanzas (or complete poems) constituting one syntactical swoop. While the stanza from the later "Coole and Ballylee, 1931" is obviously two sentences, the final one-liner alerts us to the length of the sentence preceding it, highlighting its elegant attenuation. And while the stanza is cast in ottava rima (the stanza Byron used for *Don Juan*, rhymed *abababcc*), Yeats's syntax retains the clarity of discursive prose. It travels through the intricate stanza as effortlessly as the underground river it describes.

In the stanza from "The Wild Swans at Coole" Yeats cheats a little, since the punctuation joins what could be independent clauses—clauses in which the syntax is shockingly mundane: *the trees are, the paths are, the swans are.* What's more, Yeats is working not with a highly literary stanza like ottava rima but with our most predictable stanza: the first four lines are cast in common measure, the stanza we associate with ballads and hymns—iambic tetrameter lines alternating with iambic trimeter lines. No great poem in the language begins by so dramatically relinquishing the means of verbal power.

> The **trees** are **in** their **autumn beauty**;
> The **wood**land **paths** are **dry**.

After hearing these two lines, you expect something like "This poet will write poetry / Until the day he dies." The third line disrupts our expectations. Yeats flips its initial iamb into a trochee ("**un**der"), then follows this inverted foot with an anapest, giving us three unstressed syllables in a row ("**Un**der the Oc**to**ber"). The final foot is also larded with unstressed syllables, making the whole line feel weirdly flat in a different way—not rhythmically predictable but lacking in tension: "**Un**der the Oc**to**ber **twi**light the **wa**ter." The next line begins again with a trochee and ends with a spondee ("**Mir**rors a **still sky**"), but the stanza concludes with lines that return to the mostly iambic regularity (and flaccid predication) with which the stanza began: "Up**on** the **brim**ming **wa**ter a**mong** the **stones** / Are **nine**-and-**fifty swans**." Why did Yeats go to such lengths to keep the language of "The Wild Swans at Coole" from taking flight?

The poem's diction is not as resolutely Germanic as that of "The Fish," but reinforced by the bland syntax, the bald repetitions, and the lost opportunities for rhythmic variation, it creates a soundscape in which even the smallest disruption will feel like a thunderclap. The storm breaks loose in the second line of the poem's final stanza.

> But now they drift on the still water,
> Mysterious, beautiful.

These Latinate words—*mysterious, beautiful*—are not in themselves terribly unusual or challenging, but the poem makes them feel that way. The sound of these two words, wedged together to make one elegant trimeter line, feels incantatory, revelatory, a release from the poem's almost relentlessly stolid verbal landscape. Yeats achieves the same effect in "The Tower," a sudden intrusion of Latinate diction conspiring once again with a trimeter line: "being dead, we rise, / Dream and so create / Translunar paradise."

When I was a student, I was taught to think of the plain style in English poetry as something epitomized in the Renaissance by Ben Jonson and championed more recently by poets like Yvor Winters and Thom Gunn. I was taught to think of Yeats as a poet of large-scale rhetorical effects. But no matter how arcane his cosmology, no matter how wild his thought, Yeats's sentences exhibit a restraint related to but different from the plain style. So do William Blake's.

> O Rose, thou art sick.
> The invisible worm,

That flies in the night
In the howling storm:

Has found out thy bed
Of crimson joy:
And his dark secret love
Does thy life destroy.

So do Andrew Marvell's.

What wondrous life in this I lead!
Ripe apples drop about my head;
The luscious clusters of the vine
Upon my mouth do crush their wine;
The nectarene, and curious peach,
Into my hands themselves do reach;
Stumbling on melons, as I pass,
Ensnared with flowers, I fall on grass.

What exactly do these poems have in common?

The poets I've invoked were influenced by the plain style, but each of them sits uncomfortably to the side of that tradition. Rather than fostering a poetry of direct statement, they employ extremely restrained diction in order to suggest something other than what the language of the poem also denotes, something spooky or mythic. Reading "The Sick Rose," we know immediately that this rose is an emblem for certain notions about human sexuality, though we also know it is a rose. Reading "The Wild Swans at Coole," we feel that the woods, the path, and the swans are luring us into a landscape at once physical and spiritual. The poems don't require any allegorical machinery to establish this effect: the restraint of the language itself—the immediate sense that we are being told far less than we could be told—establishes a decorum in which the clear sense of *what* is being said raises the mysterious specter of *why* it is being said.

Of the poems I've mentioned so far, Yeats's "Coole and Ballylee, 1931" is most self-conscious about this procedure: the one-line sentence that concludes its opening stanza is almost sly ("What's water but the generated soul?"), since by the time we've reached this line we've realized that, however brilliantly the poem is describing the intricate pathway of water, it's also conjuring a world elsewhere. The word *soul* rhymes tellingly with *hole*: the language of the poem rises to heaven because it cleaves to the earth.

Marvell's "The Garden" is more subtle, since its language accomplishes this heavy lifting while seeming not to flex a muscle. The very title of the poem feels at once satisfyingly concrete and at the same time immensely suggestive, and in the stanza I've quoted from the middle of the poem, we are treated to a cornucopia of sensuous detail—ripe apples, vines, nectarines, the curious peach—all of it delivered to us in lapidary couplets of seemingly effortless simplicity. But while we feel seduced by this sensual world, just as the speaker of the poem is treated to its solicitude, we feel simultaneously that we are entering translunar paradise. The wonder of the world's solicitude is unexplained, as if such gratification of our desires were utterly commonplace, and, as a result, the physical act of falling on the grass, sinking into its lusciousness, feels curiously evocative of a spiritual threshold. The wonder of the world's solicitude is unexplained, as if such gratification of our desires were utterly commonplace, and, as a result, the physical act of falling on the grass, sinking into its lusciousness, feels curiously evocative of a spiritual threshold.

The next stanza confirms this feeling.

> Meanwhile the mind, from pleasures less,
> Withdraws into its happiness:
> The mind, that ocean where each kind
> Does straight its own resemblance find,

> Yet it creates, transcending these,
> Far other worlds, and other seas,
> Annihilating all that's made
> To a green thought in a green shade.

The syntax of this poem could not be more perspicuous, the diction could not be more precise. But as in the lines by Yeats and Blake, the language feels inexplicably complex by virtue of its restraint, by virtue of implications the language raises but does not acknowledge having raised. The fifth and seventh lines are dominated by complex Latinate words (*transcending, annihilating*) while the sixth and eighth lines are made exclusively of simple Germanic words, the most important word in each line used twice: "Far other worlds, and other seas"—"To a green thought in a green shade." The diction of the final line is relentlessly monosyllabic, but its meaning feels at least as complex as the more obviously rich line preceding it. To be asked to consider the relationship of a "green thought" and a "green shade" is to feel the simple word *green* grow thick with connotation; the meaning of the line feels at once utterly plain and endlessly elusive. So does the sound. For while the Latinate word dominating the penultimate line nestles comfortably into a regular tetrameter ("Annihilating **all** that's **made**"), the final line's monosyllables disrupt it—not "To **a** green **thought** in **a** green **shade**" but "To a **green thought** in a **green shade**." Like the soul, to which the poem turns in the next stanza, this line luxuriates in the "various light."

Recently, when I happened to return to "The Garden" after many years, I discovered that everything I love about poetry is epitomized by this poem. It was as if the poem were a house I'd lived in all my life without knowing it. It was as if the poem (along with the poems I've associated with it) so determined the satisfaction I derive from poetry that the deepest act of artistic originality was inevitably an act of recapitulation, an embrace of otherness. If we all possess, as Proust suggests of Elstir, our inevitable callings, our particular rhythms, they are not original to us. The world makes us, but until we're able to wither into the limitations of ourselves, we cannot see the world.

Some of the poems that shaped me are metered and rhymed, while others are written in free verse of various kinds. In each case, what captured me was a quality of diction and syntax, a quality that our commonplace vocabulary of innovation and tradition is not well equipped to describe. In the wake of the various modernist disruptions of poetic decorum, stillness and restraint often became associated with the kind of poems we call traditional, while energy and excess were claimed by the poems we call innovative. Today, ambitious young poets write snap-crackle prose poems, while twenty years ago they wrote mordant quatrains. It's only a matter of moments before the pendulum swings back.

How crucial, then, the unprescribable exception, the poem that serves language rather than playing to taste.

> Mary in the noisy seascape
> Of the whitecaps
>
> Of another people's summer
> Talked of the theologians so brave
> In the wilderness she said and off the town pier
>
> Rounding that heavy coast of mountains
> The night drifts
> Over the rope's end
>
> Glass world
>
> Glass heaven

> Brilliant beneath the boat's round bilges
> In the surface of the water

George Oppen's diction is severely winnowed: only a handful of words derived from French or Greek (*brilliant, barnacle, theology*) disrupt this English seascape, which is dominated by nouns and phrases that sound like spondaic Anglo-Saxon kennings or compound words (*seascape, whitecaps, rope's end, glass world*). The syntax is similarly plain, its difficulties a matter not of subordination but of compression and juxtaposition. Prepositions direct us up or down. Mary is in a boat talking about theologians in the wilderness. Over the boat drifts night. Beneath the boat lies heaven. Over the land floats the breath of barnacles, and over the sea float hen coops—or at least we're tempted to see them floating there by the accumulation of unpunctuated prepositional phrases with which the poem concludes.

> Breath of the barnacles
> Over England
>
> over ocean
>
> breakwaters   hencoops

Like "The Seafarer," the Anglo-Saxon poem that Oppen inevitably invokes, "Inlet" is about finding the earth in the sky, the spiritual in the physical, and the poem's language embodies the discovery the poem describes. Working in the opposite direction from Yeats, Oppen makes the most ordinary Anglo-Saxon words sound like revelation.

> breakwaters   hencoops

The poet who rounds the "heavy coast of mountains" to see "heaven / Brilliant beneath the boat's round bilges" knows that the words *heavy* and *heaven* are derived from the same word, that *heaven* is an archaic past participle of *heave*. With its multiplicity of roots, English is one of the few European languages with different words for heaven and sky: in English, whatever is in heaven has been heaved there from the world below.

Each poem I've discussed has enacted this heavy lifting. Precision, these poems suggest, is not opposed to mystery. In fact, mystery depends on our attention to the particular nature of particular English words—on the way in which our language permits us to hear one kind of word (*big, small*) as strategically plainer and possibly even less interesting than another kind of word that means about the same thing (*immense, minute*). These kinds of choices are made in all English poems, not to mention everyday speech; but not all poems take strategic advantage of those choices, making what might otherwise seem like a retreat to stillness and restraint feel laden with connotation. "Shepherds are honest people; let them sing," said the seventeenth-century poet George Herbert, Marvell's contemporary. Misquoting this line in "Inlet" ("Shepherds are good people let them sing"), Oppen knew as well as Herbert did that rustic shepherds are notorious for saying elaborate things whenever they show up in poems. Plainness, these poets suggest, is never simple.

Neither is the road on which a poet travels to this realization, inevitable as it might seem. Although he ended his life with the dignity of Proust's Elstir, Oppen waited half a lifetime to wither into the truth of himself. As a young man, he published the preternaturally sophisticated *Discrete Series* in 1934. Then commenced a silence that didn't end until almost three decades later with the appearance of Oppen's second book, *The Materials*, in 1962. Exactly what made poems return to him seems obscure; even the explanations Oppen himself provided strike me as insufficient, and I suspect that his late withering

seemed as mysterious to him as it does to anyone else. Less obscure to me is the sense that Oppen's career magnifies what is
at stake when any writer faces the empty page, then finds it full.
More threatening is my suspicion that Oppen's complete surrender of the will to write was itself the fuel for his achievement.
Not everyone is by nature so stoic, nor does anyone need to
be—unless stoicism distinguishes him truly. My point is not
that anyone ought necessarily to strive to write like Oppen or
Marvell or any other writer. Nor is it my intention to hold up
the virtues of restraint as inevitably superior to any other virtues. "Idolatry of the forms which had inspired it," says Proust,
"a tendency to take the line of least resistance, must gradually
undermine an Elstir's progress." Which is to say that the virtue
of restraint (or anything else) cannot be guaranteed, and neither may its inevitability be assumed in a poem that does not
yet exist. Restraint will move you if such values distinguish the
poems you must write—against your own will. Yeats, Oppen,
or Marvell will matter if you learn to hear yourself by listening
to them. The greatest poems we will write already exist, and the
work of a lifetime is to recognize them as our own.

Best Thought

The time is 1917, the place London. The war is on. You are a young woman, attractive, well-off, fluent in French, German, and Italian. Since no adequate translation of Pico della Mirandola exists, you translate the Renaissance Neoplatonist's Latin yourself. But while your interest in esoteric philosophy leads you to become a member of the Hermetic Order of the Golden Dawn, your eyes are wide open. You volunteer for the Red Cross. You are immersed in London's literary avant-garde. After all, your best friend is married to the American poet Ezra Pound. Your friend's mother was once the lover of W. B. Yeats, whom Pound considers the greatest living poet— hardly an idiosyncratic opinion.

You yourself have had no love affairs of consequence. When Yeats, a fifty-one-year-old bachelor, once again proposes to Maud Gonne (the Irish actress and political activist with whom he'd fallen in love as a young man), she declines. When Yeats then proposes to Maud's daughter Iseult, she also declines; Iseult would later have an affair with Pound. A month later, when Yeats proposes to you, you accept. At 11:20 in the morning on October 20, 1917, you are married in the Harrow Road Registry Office; the witnesses are Pound and your mother.

"I think [this] girl both friendly, serviceable & very able," writes Yeats to an old friend. "She is under the glamour of a great man 30 years older than herself & with a talent for love-making," reports your mother. Honeymooning in the Ashdown Forest Hotel in Sussex, the discombobulated Yeats is writing letters to Iseult, he is writing poems: "O but her heart would break to learn my thoughts are far away." You cast a horary (an astrological chart designed to answer a particular question at a particular place and time). "Per dimandera [domandare] perche noi siamo infelice," you write in a language you know your husband does not understand—"to ask why we are unhappy."

This is one way of describing the early life of Bertha Georgie Hyde Lees Yeats, a life that would soon change dramatically. "The intellect of man is forced to choose / Perfection of the life, or of the work," wrote Yeats in "The Choice," and at times it seemed that, for him, the choice was clear. He could be an arch, distant father ("Who is it you are looking for?" he once asked his own daughter when meeting her at the family gate), a husband expert at affecting incompetence at simple everyday tasks so that his purchase on greatness might be presumed. Once, when she was worried about his eyesight, George sent him a new lamp. "What oil do I put in it?" he asked. "The lamp of course consumes lamp oil," she wrote back. "You could surely not have imagined that it demanded Sanctuary oil, or olive oil?" Easily, as George knew well, her husband could have imagined that it demanded Sanctuary oil. When she was asked how it felt to "live with a genius," George replied, "Oh alright, I never notice."

There is something wrong, something too ingeniously self-forgiving, about Yeats's distinction between perfection of the life and perfection of the work. Yeats lived in a medieval tower, he talked with dead people, he wrote some of the most beautiful lyric poems in the language. But every life is enriched by disappointment, driven by compromise, and to suggest that one might have been a good person if only one had not been a great artist is to diminish the integrity of art. It is to suggest that art is not fueled by human experience—from the aesthetic to the political to the apocalyptic—but somehow transpires beside or beyond it.

Yeats knew this couldn't be the case.

A living man is blind and drinks his drop.
What matter if the ditches are impure?
What matter if I live it all once more?
Endure that toil of growing up;
The ignominy of boyhood; the distress
Of boyhood changing into man;
The unfinished man and his pain
Brought face to face with his own clumsiness.

These lines from "A Dialogue of Self and Soul" celebrate the imperfect life, and through their effortless inhabitation of a complicated meter and rhyme scheme, they show that the most exquisite kind of artistic achievement is fueled by such imperfections. The Self speaks here, and while the Soul would argue otherwise, the Self has the last word—except inasmuch as "A Dialogue of Self and Soul" appears in *The Winding Stair* only pages away from "The Choice." Yeats arranged his poems carefully so that we might hear them doubting themselves, doubting one another, and of one thing about Yeats one may be sure: if he states a position strongly in a particular poem, he will somewhere else contradict it. Not that Yeats was facile with his thinking; far from it. In order to speak as one person, Yeats needed to be two people—in dialogue with others so that he might be in dialogue with himself.

Think back to the autumn of 1917. Stuck in the Ashdown Forest Hotel, her four-day-old marriage a disaster, George began (by her own admission) to "fake" automatic writing in order to entertain her despondent husband: she then felt her hand seized by an unseen power. Yeats described what happened next in the revised edition of *A Vision*, the esoteric account of human history and personality that the automatic writing ultimately made possible.

> What came in disjointed sentences, in almost illegible writing, was so exciting, sometimes so profound, that I persuaded her to give an hour or two day after day to the unknown writer, and after some half-dozen such hours offered to spend what remained of life explaining and piecing together those scattered sentences, "No," was the answer, "we have come to give you metaphors for poetry."

The first few days of automatic writing have not been preserved, so there is no record of Yeats being assured that the spirits had contacted him to further his poetic career. George remembered the initial contact differently: "What you have done is right for both the cat and the hare," she scribbled, confident that her husband would understand the hare as Iseult Gonne and the cat as herself, which he did. In the approximately 3,600 pages of automatic script that followed, the intimate sex life of George and Willy Yeats looms as prominently as metaphors for poetry, and while the script calls on vast reserves of esoteric knowledge, one theme is constant: if the conversations are to continue, the medium (or "interpreter," as George preferred to be called) must be satisfied. And when the interpreter is not satisfied, the script shouts it out loud and clear.

> I don't like you
> You neglect me
> You don't give me physical symbols to use

Did George and Willy really believe they were talking to dead people? Yeats began the revised version of *A Vision* by reporting a friend's comment that he seemed much better educated than he had a decade earlier; he went on to attribute this change to his and George's communications with the spirit world. Really, he ought to have attributed the change to George, whose early years of study in the British Museum fueled their conversations. George's favorite philosopher was William James, the American pragmatist who defined truth as what "works," and after Willy's death, when a scholar asked George point blank if she believed in the spirits with whom they'd conversed, she paused carefully, then said, "We thought they were expressing our best thought."

Willy's relationship to psychic phenomena alternates between a similarly tough-minded pragmatism ("metaphors for poetry") and a more tender-minded longing for a world that W. H. Auden once dismissed as "Southern Californian." Unlike his wife, Yeats could at times seem merely otherworldly, yet this quality makes his moments of direct engagement with daily life all the more moving when they do occur. "I am greatly stirred by your letter," he wrote when he learned from George that their daughter had admitted she'd neglected her schoolwork. "Most by what you quote from Anne. She could not have written like that if she was afraid of you, or if she did not want to please. There was nobody I could have written to like that. I would have been afraid to tell of my short comings."

This is the kind of thoughtful embrace of the imperfect life that one would expect of the author of poems like "A Dialogue of Self and Soul," poems that challenge their own best thinking. In the opening poem of *Responsibilities*, published three years before he married George, Yeats declares that he has "no child . . . nothing but a book" to present to his ancestors; the closing poem laments that all his "priceless things / Are but a post the passing dogs defile." Deprivation was Yeats's midlife muse, and I suspect he believed it would continue to be so. His fate seemed certain. But while he wanted a wife and child, he never imagined that this commitment to domestic life, however mediated by the assumption of male privilege, would so utterly change his thinking. The author of poems written in discouragement was liberated to doubt himself more strenuously, and he became the author of poems written in ecstasy, poems borne of an uncanny imaginative confidence unseen in English poetry since Blake.

> The darkness drops again; but now I know
> That twenty centuries of stony sleep
> Were vexed to nightmare by a rocking cradle,
> And what rough beast, its hour come round at last,
> Slouches towards Bethlehem to be born?

It wasn't just the automatic writing that made these concluding lines of "The Second Coming" possible; the sensibility of the later poems feels more like George than Willy—fascinated by the world beyond the senses, but also skeptical, tough-minded, embedded in the earth.

The final sentence of "The Second Coming" is a question: just as the shape of twenty centuries was determined by the birth of Jesus, so will the tenor of the next age be determined by a similarly momentous birth—but of what? The uncertainty is riveting, and the temptation to read the poem as prophetic condemnation is intense. But when we turn the page to "A Prayer for My Daughter" in *Michael Robartes and the Dancer*, the book in which "The Second Coming" was carefully placed, Yeats asks us to doubt the metaphors that constitute the prophecy.

> Once more the storm is howling, and half hid
> Under this cradle-hood and coverlid

> My child sleeps on. There is no obstacle
> But Gregory's wood and one bare hill
> Whereby the haystack- and roof-leveling wind,
> Bred on the Atlantic, can be stayed;
> And for an hour I have walked and prayed
> Because of the great gloom that is in my mind.

With these lines we are suddenly dropped from prophetic to domestic utterance: the apocalyptic cradle of "The Second Coming" becomes the simple cradle in which a particular child, Anne Yeats, is sleeping. There is no violence in the street; the weather is bad. A father is worrying about the safety of his child. Does the future look grim simply because a sleeping baby looks vulnerable, because a storm is blowing off the Atlantic? Or does the future look grim because the human mind, trapped in its own "great gloom," imposes immense metaphorical significance on these ordinary events, events that happen every night, not just at the inauguration of a new age?

The questions provoked by "A Prayer for My Daughter" send us back to "The Second Coming." Notice how its final stanza begins: having declared so charismatically in the first stanza that "things fall apart," the prophetic voice begins to interpret its own declarations—but not very carefully.

> Surely some revelation is at hand;
> Surely the Second Coming is at hand.
> The Second Coming! Hardly are those words out
> When a vast image out of *Spiritus Mundi*
> Troubles my sight.

These lines embody the slippery process by which observation becomes prophecy. In the first line the voice insists that "surely" these events portend "some" revelation—it doesn't know what revelation. In the second line the voice suddenly suggests that this revelation must be the Second Coming, and the reiteration of the syntactical pattern ("surely . . . is at hand") makes this quick association sound considered. The voice even registers its own surprise at this association ("The Second Coming!")— as if the poem doesn't actually consider its titular subject until it's half over. After these words tumble from the mouth of the speaker, as if from the mouth of a medium unworthy of the title interpreter, the stanza abandons its shaky logic for a confident vision of the world's fate.

> Somewhere in sands of the desert
> A shape with lion body and the head of a man,
> A gaze blank and pitiless as the sun,
> Is moving its slow thighs, while all about it
> Reel shadows of the indignant desert birds.
> The darkness drops again; but now I know
> That twenty centuries of stony sleep
> Were vexed to nightmare by a rocking cradle,
> And what rough beast, its hour come round at last,
> Slouches towards Bethlehem to be born?

No longer is this voice speculating that "some" revelation is at hand. "Now I know," says the voice, but what exactly does it know? On what evidence does this knowledge depend? The phrase "rough beast" is powerfully suggestive because it is also (as I've suggested of Yeats's diction at large) strategically plain, provocatively monosyllabic, and our attitude toward this obscure apocalyptic figure is largely determined by the brilliantly precise verb *slouches*. To imagine that our unknowable fate "slouches" toward us suggests a great deal more about our state of expectation than about future events.

"The Second Coming" was provoked by Yeats's acute sense of

the violence and uncertainty of Europe during the First World War and the subsequent civil war in Ireland, but the poem does not simply render a judgment (though it is often quoted as if it did). "The Second Coming" is a dramatization of the route through which a mind might come, responsibly or irresponsibly, to apocalyptic conclusions in response to violence and uncertainty. Yeats was at times attracted to the rhetoric of apocalypse, but in "The Second Coming" he is as troubled by the need to leap to conclusions as he is by a chaotic world that may (or may not) support them. To read the poem in conjunction with "A Prayer for My Daughter," as Yeats asks us to do, first allows us to see that the poems question each other. Then we may see that "The Second Coming" doubts itself, turning against what might initially seem to be its own best thought.

This is how Yeats's poems work. Often he rewrote his poems long after they were initially published, but he was not a compulsive reviser like Auden or Marianne Moore, poets who tried over a lifetime to get the poem right; Yeats wanted to discover something unprecedented, something that could never merely be willed, in the act of remaking his language. And neither did the poems settle easily into themselves once Yeats was finished with them. His goal was to make the poems embody the dialectical process by which they were made. Interrogating each other, the poems interrogate themselves, making individual poems feel double.

> All that I have said and done,
> Now that I am old and ill,

he wrote in "Man and the Echo," one of his last poems,

> Turns into a question till
> I lie awake night after night
> And never get the answers right.

These lines sound frustrated, but they are driven by joy, the joy of having more to say, the language of each conclusion transformed into a fresh question.

Yeats's language seems to me as challenging today as it was a hundred years ago, but recently, in a review of one American poet by another, I found this sentence: "Yeats may be a distant and unlikely model for contemporary poets." Why? Because he arranged syllables into rhythms? Because he doesn't live in Brooklyn? Yeats did not write poems by attempting consciously to distinguish himself from his forebears. Nor did he write poems because he married a complicated, intelligent woman or because he engaged in psychical research. Many people might find satisfaction in such things. Others might find them quaint.

A few people might also take hard-won satisfaction in rhyming their own name with the word "slates," in rhyming their wife's name with the word "forge," in arranging a single sentence into four iambic tetrameter lines whose rhythmic density asks (as the title of the poem suggests) "To Be Carved on a Stone at Thoor Ballylee."

> I, the poet William Yeats,
> With old mill boards and sea-green slates,
> And smithy work from the Gort forge,
> Restored this tower for my wife George.

Less Than Everything

W hat did Chinese poetry sound like to speakers of English at the end of the nineteenth century, when Yeats was writing his first great poems?

> O fair white silk, fresh from the weaver's loom,
> Clear as the frost, bright as the winter snow—
> See! friendship fashions out of thee a fan,
> Round as the round moon shines in heaven above,
> At home, abroad, a close companion thou,
> Stirring at every move the grateful gale.
> And yet I fear, ah me! that autumn chills
> Cooling the dying summer's torrid rage,
> Will see thee laid neglected on the shelf,
> All thoughts of bygone days, like them bygone.

This translation, by Herbert Giles, sounds like a mockery of Chinese poetry. But when the translation was made, a poem needed to be metered if it was going to be recognized by most people as a poem. Giles's march of iambs is a far cry from the rhythmical delicacy of early Yeats.

In 1914 Ezra Pound made what seems like a translation of the same poem. In fact, it is an adaptation of Giles's translation. Without any knowledge of Chinese, without any literal trot, with nothing but Giles's clumsy pentameters to work from, Pound produced this poem, called "Fan-Piece, for Her Imperial Lord."

> O fan of white silk,
>> Clear as the frost on the grass-blade,
> You also are laid aside.

If this translation does not sound to us like a mockery of Chinese poetry, it is because Pound invented the poetic idiom with which we now associate Chinese poetry; if the poem is in any way more scrupulously attuned to the letter or spirit of the original poem, the accuracy is purely an accident. As T. S. Eliot once remarked, Pound is the inventor of Chinese poetry in the English language. How and why did that invention take place?

Recall Pound's three famous principles for writing an imagist poem.

1. Direct treatment of the "thing" whether subjective or objective.
2. To use absolutely no word that does not contribute to the presentation.
3. As regarding rhythm: to compose in the sequence of the musical phrase, not in sequence of the metronome.

Although Pound knew that Giles's translation was badly written, he nonetheless saw something with which he could work, and he produced his version of "Fan-Piece" as if by feeding the translation into a computer programmed with imagist principles. To compose in the sequence of the musical phrase: not "O fair white silk, fresh from the weaver's loom" but "O fan of white silk." Direct treatment of the thing: not "Clear as the frost, bright as the winter snow" but "Clear as the frost on the grass-blade." To use absolutely no word that does not contribute to the presentation: not

> And yet I fear, ah me! that autumn chills
> Cooling the dying summer's torrid rage,
> Will see thee laid neglected on the shelf

but

> You also are laid aside.

If Pound's poem possesses a dreamlike intensity, it is because, as Freud pointed out, dreams work by compression: our thoughts are reduced to sensations.

Pound once admitted that his most famous imagist poem, "In a Station of the Metro," began as a poem of thirty lines from which he distilled his famous couplet: the poem depended upon the same editorial acumen that allowed Pound to carve "Fan-Piece" from Giles's translation. But whether the imagist poems were actually compressed from longer poems or not, they inevitably give the impression of having been compressed. The aura of the unsaid is always palpable, and that aura is the poem's tone. And without an immediately identifiable tone, a highly compressed poem would seem merely thin or perplexing, not enticing or seductive, given its dearth of narrative information.

What exactly do we mean by tone? The most semantically charged word in "Fan-Piece" is *also*—"You also are laid aside." The word suggests that the speaker of the poem shares the fate of the fan, and, more than that, the word acknowledges a general sense of human ephemerality, a woeful recognition that everyone will one day be laid aside. But the tone of the poem— the effect of the poem's sonic patterning—is not woeful. The poem's terse, unenjambed lines, each of them weighted by adjacent stressed syllables ("white silk"—"grass-blade"), create a soundscape of controlled dignity, a tone that tells us as much as or more than the meaning of the word *also*. "Fan-Piece" feels riven with loss because the poem sounds stoically uninvolved with the emotional repercussions of loss.

Like any achievement in art, however, this one entails crucial limitations. The compression of Pound's imagist poems, fueled by tone, has in many ways determined the direction of poetry in our language for the past hundred years, and it has done so most crucially by precluding expansion or dilation. The prescriptions that produced imagist poems made no mention of length, but the second of Pound's "don'ts"—"to use absolutely no word that does not contribute to the presentation"—inevitably encouraged a discipline that shied away from the discursive presentation of information, shrinking lyric utterance to its pithiest core. How then could a poet write a long poem at all, a poem that could be seen as a successor to *The Prelude, In Memoriam,* and *Leaves of Grass?* How could Pound write a poem of immense length while at the same time preserving the compressed lyric intensity that distinguishes poems like "Fan-Piece" and "In a Station of the Metro"?

Pound's ultimate answer to this question would be the *Cantos,* the long poem on which he labored for half a century. But his first answer to this question was "Villanelle: The Psychological Hour," published in 1915. The poem begins with these lines.

> I had over-prepared the event,
> > that much was ominous.
> With middle-ageing care
> > I had laid out just the right books.
> I had almost turned down the pages.
>
> *Beauty is so rare a thing.*
> *So few drink of my fountain.*

So much barren regret,
So many hours wasted!
And now I watch, from the window,
        the rain, the wandering busses.

"Their little cosmos is shaken"—
        the air is alive with that fact.
In their parts of the city
        they are played on by diverse forces.
How do I know?
        Oh, I know well enough.
For them there is something afoot.
        As for me;
I had over-prepared the event—

    Beauty is so rare a thing.
    So few drink of my fountain.

Two friends: a breath of the forest . . .
Friends? Are people less friends
        because one has just, at last, found them?

Why is this poem, which is not a villanelle, called "Villanelle: The Psychological Hour"? Pound had something to say about everything, and in an essay published in the same year as his poem, he said that the villanelle achieves its greatest intensity when "the refrains are an emotional fact, which the intellect, in the various gyrations of the poem, tries in vain and in vain to escape." This is how the repetition of the line "I had over-prepared the event" functions: no matter how culpable the friends, how shaken their cosmos, the speaker must admit again that he had overprepared the event. But the repetition of the couplet feels different—not so much a part of the unfolding emotional drama of the poem as an interruption of it, and the interruptions pace the poem: *"Beauty is so rare a thing. / So few drink of my fountain."* We may not yet have an inkling of what the lines mean in relationship to the rest of the poem, but the lines are in themselves utterly clear, and their reappearance reassures us that a previously submerged structure is rising to the surface of the poem.

Reassures us, yet stymies us, since this structural principle disappears from "Villanelle: The Psychological Hour" after its first section: the concluding two sections dwindle away, each one more compressed than the one preceding it.

> Now the third day is here—
> > no word from either;
> No word from her nor him,
> Only another man's note:
> > "Dear Pound, I am leaving England."

This final section of "Villanelle: The Psychological Hour" tempts us with a new structural principle, one we apply retrospectively. Reading the phrase "Now the third day is here," we postulate a buried narrative: this poem is about someone being stood up by two friends, a man and a woman, on three successive days. But rather than solidifying our experience of the poem, this narrative begs more questions. Who are that man and woman? Why have the meetings been planned? Why have they been postponed? None of these questions are answered. What then holds the fragmentary pieces of "Villanelle: The Psychological Hour" together while still allowing them to feel like fragments that aspire to the lyric purity of the imagist poem? What allows a highly compressed poem to feel complete when so many of its expectations for continuity and closure are not fulfilled?

The answer once again is tone, which in the absence of narrative information is as crucial to this forty-three-line poem as it is to the three-line "Fan-Piece." Even when "Villanelle: The Psychological Hour" asks questions, its flat, unenjambed, syntactically complete lines create a tone of unruffled control: "I had over-prepared the event"—"For them there is something afoot"—"Only another man's note." The poem sustains its sonic composure in the face of an onslaught of inexplicable experience, and the shock of the final line, in which Pound shatters this tone by naming himself, depends on the fact that the information presented earlier in the poem feels inadequate or even irrelevant. If we knew what event had been overprepared, if we knew the identity of the man and the woman, if we knew where there had been dancing, then the uneasy thrill of the poem's most blatantly referential line would disappear.

Dear Pound, I am leaving England.

As we process that line, our experience of the poem mirrors the experience described in the poem. We feel intimate with what we do not fully comprehend—a feeling that is commonplace in human life, conspicuously in dreams, but rare in our experience of art because we expect to be the master of the poem we read. Mystery, says this poem, is a far more human condition than mastery. And mystery, which depends on clarity, is the opposite of confusion.

"Villanelle: The Psychological Hour" is by no means the first poem to be made from a concatenation of shorter poems. But in *Leaves of Grass* and *In Memoriam*, each poem in the sequence, however brief, feels like a complete utterance, a poem that may be comprehended whole. Even if we haven't read any of the sections preceding it, we don't feel the absence of crucial information when we read the seventh of the 131 sections of *In Memoriam*, Tennyson's elegy for Arthur Hallam, a friend who died in 1833.

Dark house, by which once more I stand
  Here in the long unlovely street,
  Doors, where my heart was used to beat
So quickly, waiting for a hand,

A hand that can be clasp'd no more—
  Behold me, for I cannot sleep,
  And like a guilty thing I creep
At earliest morning to the door.

He is not here; but far away
  The noise of life begins again,
  And ghastly through the drizzling rain
On the bald street breaks the blank day.

The opening eight-line sentence of this poem dumps all of its sonic shimmer ("the long unlovely street") onto the second sentence, whose four bald syllables have none: "He is not here." What we feel in those four syllables is the absence of tone, and we experience that absence as a thrill because the long sentence preceding it is in contrast so tonally luxurious. And because syntax conspires so elegantly with tonal shift, we feel that this poem completes its action, and when we reach the end of the poem, the welter of stressed syllables underscores that feeling: "On the **bald street breaks** the **blank day**."

But while tone shifts crucially, this shift does not bear much structural weight: information also guides us through the poem. By capitalizing on tone as a structural principle in the absence of much information, in contrast, Pound made a more highly compressed long poem possible. Ultimately, he made possible the *Cantos*, but most immediately, he made possible *The Waste Land*, on whose final organization he worked with Eliot during the winter of 1921.

There is shadow under this red rock,
(Come in under the shadow of this red rock),
And I will show you something different from either
Your shadow at morning striding behind you
Or your shadow at evening rising to meet you;
I will show you fear in a handful of dust.
>   *Frisch weht der Wind*
>   *Der Heimat zu*
>   *Mein Irisch Kind,*
>   *Wo weilest du?*
"You gave me hyacinths first a year ago;
"They called me the hyacinth girl."
—Yet when we came back, late, from the Hyacinth garden,
Your arms full, and your hair wet, I could not
Speak, and my eyes failed, I was neither
Living nor dead, and I knew nothing,
Looking into the heart of light, the silence.
Oed' und leer das Meer.

This passage from *The Waste Land* begins with lines in a strongly prophetic tone, reminiscent of Ezekiel. But these lines are immediately superseded by four lines in German: their sound is radically at odds with what we have just heard, though if we know their source (a sailor's melancholy song to his beloved from Wagner's *Tristan und Isolde*), the lines seem continuous with the passage that follows, the recollection of lost erotic promise in the hyacinth garden. This passage, though very brief, contains just enough narrative material to make it feel like a complete scene. But however explicable the passage may be, the "I" who speaks it bears no obvious relationship to the "I" who would show us fear in a handful of dust. Nor does this "I" seem continuous with the speaker of the lines that follow:

with the swift introduction of Madame Sosostris, we jump from the heartbroken ("I knew nothing") to the broadly comic ("Madame Sosostris, famous clairvoyante, / Had a bad cold"), only to find that the tone of these lines not only contrasts with what we've heard so far but is itself interrupted by a different tone, suddenly lyrical and achingly sincere: "Those are pearls that were his eyes"—a line lifted from Ariel's song to Ferdinand in *The Tempest*.

We may not yet understand why these various fragments are juxtaposed, but we have little doubt about what the fragments are saying, just as we have little doubt when we are reading "Villanelle: The Psychological Hour." But while the tone of Pound's poem shifts decisively in its final line ("Dear Pound, I am leaving England"), the tone of *The Waste Land* shifts constantly from precision to precision: "Come in under the shadow of this red rock"—"You gave me hyacinths first a year ago"—"*Oed' und leer das Meer*"—"Madame Sosostris, famous clairvoyante." Even the tone of a line in a language we may not understand feels precise: the phrase "*Oed' und leer das Meer*" is far more sonically provocative than the phrase "desolate and empty the sea," which translates it. *The Waste Land* grows coherent not because we're encouraged to look for continuities of narrative or character but because we're guided by this extraordinary clarity of tone. It is, in a sense, the longest lyric cry in our language.

Recall the question implicit in "Fan-Piece, for Her Imperial Lord": how can one write a long poem without sacrificing the unrelieved intensity of a highly compressed poem? "Villanelle: The Psychological Hour" offered a tentative answer to that question, but by reducing more drastically the reliance on narrative and by capitalizing more aggressively on shifts of tone, *The Waste Land* offered the definitive answer. Prior to *The Waste Land*, no poem of such length had ever been organized in this way, but since the publication of *The Waste Land*, many poems have been organized this way, not least the *Cantos*, to which Pound returned with renewed energy after collaborating with Eliot. How far can these procedures be pushed? How much compression can the medium of poetry withstand while still offering the poet enough tools to structure a poem of any length?

Consider the last of the thirteen sections of Susan Howe's "Silence Wager Stories."

> Lies are stirring storms
> I listen spheres from far
> Whereunder shoreward away
> you walked here Protector
> unassuaged asunder thought
> you walked here Overshadow
> I listen spheres of stars
> I draw you close ever so
> Communion come down and down
> Quiet place to stop here
> Who knows ever no one knows
> to know unlove no forgive

Why is this poem, which tells no stories, called "Silence Wager Stories"? The poem does refer to two powerful narratives about the relationship of love and death. "Who go down to hell alive / is the theme of this work," says Howe with disarming forthrightness in the poem's opening section, alluding to the story of Orpheus, who fails to rescue the dead Eurydice from hell. "Loveless and sleepless the sea," says Howe more enigmatically in the poem's epilogue, translating the line from Wagner's *Tristan und Isolde* that Eliot quotes in *The Waste Land*. Tristan and Isolde could love each other only in death.

But having invoked these narratives, Howe's poem does not dwell on them. Like *The Waste Land* and "Villanelle: The Psychological Hour," "Silence Wager Stories" does contain bits of narrative information; but like Eliot and Pound, Howe is careful not to let these bits of information structure her poem, which is resolutely lyric in demeanor. Relieving us from responsibility for searching for a coherent narrative, voice, or even syntax, she consequently liberates us into an unmitigated attention to tone. What does Orpheus do after he loses Eurydice a second time? He sings. What does Isolde do as she joins Tristan in death? She sings.

Susan Howe's songs are muted, murmured, clenched, constricted—as if the principles of compression and juxtaposition that underlie *The Waste Land* had reduced the poem's constituent parts from brief passages to single lines. But in contrast to Eliot's, Howe's juxtapositions are less flamboyant, her tonal range more subdued. Because there seems only occasionally to be any syntactical relationship between the lines ("I listen spheres of stars / I draw you close ever so"), and because the continuities of sound often feel more powerful than the continuities of sense ("Lies are stirring storms / I listen spheres from far"), and because discontinuity of sound is more prominent than such continuities ("you walked here Protector / unassuaged asunder thought"), the dominant tone of the poem is resolute, dignified, cold. It registers the pressure of human feeling—grief—through the act of managing or containing it.

The poem's epilogue consequently feels like an eruption: its rich lyricism, driven by syntactical and lexical repetition, stands at odds with the poem's stalwart refusal not only of narrative but also of syntactical and even sonic continuity.

> Half thought thought otherwise
> loveless and sleepless the sea

Where you are where I would be
half thought thought otherwise
Loveless and sleepless the sea

Consider that final line, translated from Wagner via Eliot. My literal translation of the line from Wagner is toneless: "desolate and empty the sea." It sounds like a line in a Herbert Giles poem: "I think that I shall always be / Desolate and empty as the sea." By creating in contrast an intricate pattern of repeated vowels and consonants ("Loveless and sleepless the sea"), Howe is establishing a continuity of tone. The sound of the word *loveless* delivers us to the word *sleepless* and the word *sleep* delivers us to the word *sea*. Then, seduced by this pattern of repeated sounds, we are further seduced by the repetition of the line, matched with the repetition of another line ("half thought thought otherwise") that also repeats itself internally, the syntax arranged in a chiasmic or mirror-image pattern. Within this swirling space of sonic, lexical, and syntactical repetition, a space of Tennysonian richness, the line "Where you are where I would be" is the center, the still point. The sound of the words directs us to this line, which also repeats itself internally, and we glimpse there the possibility of what another kind of poem would present as a thematic center. The poem says: where you are (dead) is where I (alive) would be. I am Orpheus, singing low, but I would rather be Isolde, singing in order to be silenced, joined with you forever in death. The poem is an elegy for David von Schlegell, an American sculptor who died in 1992.

Poems are not necessarily songs, but all poets make works of art that, whatever else they do, seduce us from their beginnings to their ends through the simultaneous construction and dismantling of a pattern of sounds. The tonal control apparent in Howe, Eliot, and Pound is also fully apparent in *In Memoriam;*

Tennyson had one of the finest ears among poets in our language. Tone was for him one tool among several, however, and in a more highly compressed long poem, in the strategic absence of narrative, character, voice, argument, or syntax itself, tone is what guides us through the poem.

Every poem exists by virtue of the power of what it is not. But while the seductiveness of radical compression may ask us to wonder about the seductiveness of an equally radical attenuation, the virtue of compression feels difficult to second-guess. Reading poems, we expect the language to hold our attention because the syllables create dense patterns of sound; writing poems, we listen for those lines that lack density, and we either cut them or revise them. How then do we recognize the work of lines that flirt with what we might otherwise call bad writing? How do we describe that work? One answer to these questions begins with the poet generally thought of as the greatest in our language.

Writing Badly

At the beginning of Shakespeare's tragedy, King Lear invites his three daughters to tell him which one loves him best. While Cordelia refuses to play along, responding with compressed intensity ("Nothing, my lord"), Regan and Goneril serve up the hyperbole their father demands, their sentiment becoming increasingly vapid to the degree that its language is elaborated.

> Sir, I love you more than word can wield the matter;
> Dearer than eyesight, space, and liberty;
> Beyond what can be valued, rich or rare;
> No less than life, with grace, health, beauty, honor;
> As much as child e'er loved, or father found.

Listening to this protracted utterance, we learn to distrust the character before we know anything about her. We hear the elaboration not as invention but as strategy, a lack of meaningful interiority. We feel an overpowering motivation but a paucity of means.

For what reasons would an artist court such lack in a lyric poem, evading the discipline of compression, as Elizabeth Bishop does in the opening stanza of "Brazil, January 1, 1502"?

> Januaries, Nature greets our eyes
> exactly as she must have greeted theirs:
> every square inch filling in with foliage—

> big leaves, little leaves, and giant leaves,
> blue, blue-green, and olive,
> with occasional lighter veins and edges,
> or a satin underleaf turned over;
> monster ferns
> in silver-gray relief,
> and flowers, too, like giant water lilies
> up in the air—up, rather, in the leaves—
> purple, yellow, two yellows, pink,
> rust red and greenish white.

How could you tell, outside of the context of this poem, that the lines "purple, yellow, two yellows, pink, / rust red and greenish white" are any good? The poem wants to get something right; there isn't just one yellow here, there are two yellows. But the discrimination feels unmotivated, elaborated to the brink of boredom. Why should we care that there are two yellows? Why should we be interested in the unspecified generality of "Nature" at all? Lacking the intensity we usually associate with poetic language, Bishop's words feel like stretch socks, one size fits all. Why then do we suspect we're reading a great poem?

The seductiveness of lassitude is initially easier to describe in music and film, arts that inhabit their temporal processes more viscerally than poetry does. I'm thinking of the lovers' long and tediously dispassionate kiss beside the railroad tracks in Antonioni's *L'Avventura*. Or the moment near the conclusion of the thirty-first piano sonata, opus 110, when Beethoven slowly repeats a G major chord ten times in a row. Such moments feel weirdly flat, prolix, or dilatory. Inhabiting them, we become aware of the mundanity of the artistic medium, rather than feeling that the simplest means have been raised to a higher power. We feel as if the work of art has not just slowed down but abandoned its own temporal realm in order to inhabit for a moment the world of real time, the time in which we're watching or listening or reading.

Renaissance rhetoricians spoke of the virtues and potential dangers of *dilation* or *amplification*, by which they meant to describe the strategic elaboration of a simple effect. This is what Othello means when, asked how he wooed Desdemona, he says that he "would all my pilgrimage dilate" in order to "draw from her a prayer of earnest heart." Goneril's speech in *King Lear* embraces the mere loquaciousness against which rhetoricians warned, but in "The Eve of St. Agnes" Keats makes the potential seductiveness of dilation explicit. He shifts our gaze from the beloved's body to the sensual world arranged to seduce her, quickening our investment in narrative and erotic fulfillment by delaying it with a purposefully detailed appeal to sight, touch, taste, smell, and, most importantly (through the gorgeous patterning of the language), sound.

> And still she slept an azure-lidded sleep,
> In blanched linen, smooth, and lavender'd,
> While he from forth the closet brought a heap
> Of candied apple, quince, and plum, and gourd;
> With jellies soother than the creamy curd,
> And lucent syrops, tinct with cinnamon;
> Manna and dates, in argosy transferr'd
> From Fez; and spiced dainties, every one,
> From silken Samarcand to cedar'd Lebanon.

Othello dilates in order to seduce his beloved; Keats dilates in order to involve his reader in the act of seduction that his poem recounts. But in contrast to these moments, the moments I describe in Beethoven, Antonioni, and Bishop muddle any narrative or erotic economy in which delay increases the pleasure of closure or gratification. The longer they last, the more these moments cease to promise fullness and instead feel provocatively like emptiness, as if the artist had dozed off, forgetting to move the camera or shift his hands. And while such moments feel ancillary to what we would describe as the central events of the works of art containing them, the power of these works of art would be greatly diminished if such moments were simply jettisoned. How can we say with any certainty that the slow repetition of a G major chord is brilliant or boring? It's easy to say that the phrase "candied apple, quince, and plum" is more compelling than "big leaves, little leaves, and giant leaves," but should it be?

Necessary at this stage of my argument is a rehearsal of a kind of modernist taste, the kind that, as we've seen, prizes compression and elision. Recall the imagist Pound proclaiming that a good poem contains "absolutely no word that does not contribute to the presentation." Compare this highly compressed passage from the final movement of *The Waste Land*—

> What is the city over the mountains
> Cracks and reforms and bursts in the violet air
> Falling towers
> Jerusalem Athens Alexandria
> Vienna London
> Unreal

—with a passage from "The Dry Salvages," the third of the *Four Quartets*, written twenty years later. The quartets contain scattered moments of compressed intensity, but these moments are set against passages of rhythmically flaccid and imagistically imprecise writing—passages that, in the context of the quartets ultimately feel more unsettling than the intensities.

It seems, as one becomes older,
That the past has another pattern, and ceases to be a mere
    sequence—
Or even development: the latter a partial fallacy,
Encouraged by superficial notions of evolution,
Which becomes, in the popular mind, a means of disown-
    ing the past.
The moments of happiness—not the sense of well-being,
Fruition, fulfillment, security or affection,
Or even a very good dinner, but the sudden illumination—
We had the experience but missed the meaning,
And approach to the meaning restores the experience
In a different form, beyond any meaning
We can assign to happiness. I have said before
That the past experience revived in the meaning
Is not the experience of one life only
But of many generations.

One can imagine how quickly Pound's blue pencil would have
excised this passage from *The Waste Land*, the phrase "even a
very good dinner" pushing him probably into despair. Many
of Eliot's readers, schooled in the unmitigated intensities of
The Waste Land itself, did despair, for like the repetition of the
G major chord in Beethoven's opus 110 or the attenuated kiss in
L'Avventura, this passage from "The Dry Salvages" is, by modernist standards, unacceptably leisurely. The diction is imprecise, the
lines larded with unstressed syllables, the tone egregiously reassuring—the tone of an adult speaking to a child whose acumen
the adult may not recognize: "It seems, as one becomes older, /
That the past has another pattern, and ceases to be a mere sequence— / Or even development." To begin the passage with "it
seems" is to announce an inability to describe how it is or even

what it is. The words *sequence* and *development* don't seem different enough to justify the elaboration of the former by the latter, so the passage feels unmotivated. It moves forward by equivocation, dulling rather than sharpening the distinctions for which it gropes: "I have said before."

Even before Eliot's speaker tells us he's repeating himself, we recognize that the passage glosses lines from "East Coker," the quartet preceding "The Dry Salvages."

> Not the intense moment
> Isolated, with no before and after,
> But a lifetime burning in every moment
> And not the lifetime of one man only
> But of old stones that cannot be deciphered.

Compared to the dilatory lines from "The Dry Salvages," these lines possess a more immediately recognizable authority: the tone is oracular, the diction concretely imagistic rather than generalized, the lineation marked by enjambment ("intense moment / Isolated") that energizes the syntax. Rather than meandering through a loose accumulation of appositions ("not the sense of well-being, / Fruition, fulfillment, security or affection"), this sentence feels driven by an argument ("Not the intense moment / Isolated, with no before and after, / But a lifetime"), and the sentence reinforces the argument by repeating its syntactical pattern ("not the lifetime of one man only / But of old stones").

The design of the quartets embodies this argument, for if *The Waste Land* is a poem of intense moments with no before and after, then *Four Quartets* is a poem that aspires to occupy the temporal space of ordinary human behavior, reserving the occupation of the timeless moment for the saint. Each of the quartets begins with an account of a moment of heightened spiritual awareness; each moment is associated with a particular place, and the work of the poem is to recognize the necessity of what may initially seem like the "waste sad time" that human beings inevitably inhabit between their rare experiences of timeless moments.

But while the passage I've quoted from "East Coker" describes the need for something other than the timeless moment, the passage from "The Dry Salvages" embodies that need in language that repeats a now familiar point in strategically familiar language. Rather than feeling uniquely central to the poem, the passage feels as though it were standing beside the poem, explicating it, repeating its more self-consciously inevitable gestures in a language of generality—a language we associate not with the aesthetic space created by great poems but with the space surrounding poems, the space in which we speak and breathe, the space in which we're free to repeat ourselves, foraging for alternatives, rather than mustering the singularity we associate with art. Taken out of context, the passage may sound weirdly flat; in context, we experience the passage as an eschewal of artifice—an unexpected recovery of a world we thought we had to abandon in order to purchase the pleasure of art.

Context is all. Crucial to the effect of the repeated G major chord in Beethoven's opus 110 is the fact that this sonata is written in the key of A-flat major: G major is as far from home as the tonal system allows Beethoven to venture, yet he dwells there, seemingly uninterested in resolution. Crucial to the effect of the dispassionate kiss in *L'Avventura* is that its embarrassingly tedious duration does not lead to consummation but is finally interrupted by a speeding train. And crucial to the effect of Eliot's passages of flattened writing is their relationship to other kinds of writing within the quartets. The passages are not, like this line from elsewhere in "The Dry Salvages," epigrammatically precise, therefore charismatic.

> Time is no healer; the patient is no longer here.

Neither are they, like these lines, imagistically concrete, therefore oracular.

> The salt is on the briar rose,
> The fog is in the fir trees.

When the writing turns charismatic or oracular—when suddenly the train speeds past, when the key of A-flat major is quickly reestablished—we feel the intervention of urgency. But while urgency is welcome, it is not automatically thrilling. The effect of the dilation in the *Quartets* is not simply a matter of what Roland Barthes called the "dilatory space" on which the pleasure of narrative gratification depends; neither is it a matter of what James Wright called "prose lines" in poems, lines of lesser intensity that create a backdrop or launching pad for rhetorically heightened lines. The effect of dilation feels at once most powerful and most tenuous if, once the train speeds past, as trains are after all given to do, the doldrums of G major feel in retrospect curiously enticing.

Enticing is potentially a misleading word, however, for such moments must also continue to feel unsettling, unjustifiably flat. While the power of Eliot's enervated writing depends on context, that power is also contingent on a challenge to context: dilation may threaten to last so long that we forget the possible intervention of necessity—forget the very context on which the power of such passages also depends. In *King Lear*, Goneril's dilatory speech doesn't challenge us in quite this way; dramatic necessity motivates her otherwise unnecessary verbiage. But compare Goneril's protracted expression of love for her father to the kind of protracted speaking we hear later in *King Lear* from Kent, Edgar, and Lear himself. When Kent is asked simply to identify himself, he says,

> I do profess to be no less than I seem, to serve him
> truly that will put me in trust, to love him that
> is honest, to converse with him that is wise and
> says little, to fear judgment, to fight when I cannot
> choose, and to eat no fish.

Outcast, speaking in disguise to the outcast Lear, Kent insists that he can "deliver a plain message bluntly," but he does anything but that. Though Goneril's speech is unnecessarily elaborated, it sets a dramatic action swiftly in motion. Kent's speech not only stalls the engine; his language dismantles the grammatical rails on which necessity runs while at the same time riding on them, and his rambling verbosity feels as inexplicable yet as charismatic to us as it does to his auditors. To be no less than one seems is to eat no fish: who could disagree?

Shakespeare became a master of this more unstable species of dilation. Recall the gravedigger's scene in *Hamlet* or the knocking-at-the-gate scene in *Macbeth*, scenes that interrupt actions of propulsive inevitability, yanking us out of the revved-up space of art and dropping us back into the apparently inconsequential space in which we exist, as if we turned away from the drama to have a conversation about grocery shopping. When such scenes are most effective, they leave us feeling unsettled, not just relieved or hungry for what's next. The audience of *King Lear* craves a release from the play's harsh economy of necessity, in which nothing comes from nothing and something from something. And yet the release offered by Kent's behavior doesn't console easily or permanently. Is his speech desperate or determined, a lapse or a reprieve?

By the time Shakespeare was writing, there was already an established tradition not only of describing dilation but also of discriminating between plausible and implausible versions of it. But by the time Eliot was writing the *Four Quartets*, the impulse that led him to entertain the aesthetic function of flaccid writing had become controversial in a more particular way. Once romanticism generated its inevitable successor in modernism, a modernism that prized compression and elision, then lassitude became something more inevitably to be scorned. This development obscured the longer history of aesthetic choices, making alternatives seem mutually exclusive. And since Eliot was the twentieth century's most influential opponent of dilation in *The Waste Land* before he became its most elegant exemplar in *Four Quartets*, the sound of lassitude became an especially charged aspect of Eliot's legacy.

But if "The Dry Salvages" is in these terms a postmodern poem, one that invites us to consider its relationship to modernism, it is more importantly a poem that encourages us to imagine art as a continuous struggle over the past few centuries, rather than over the past few decades. In the short-term history of taste, dilation comes in and out of style; the power of works of art embracing it depends on works of art that dismiss it with equal vigor. In the long-term history of art, these oppositions fall away, relieving us from the pressure to narrow the field of artistic expression. *Four Quartets* offers that relief, for instead of upending modernism's disdain for dilation, the poem reestablishes its place within the context of a variety of aesthetic choices—one of many effects to which an artist might aspire, as Shakespeare and Beethoven did. The poem bequeaths these choices to later poems, as it received them from earlier ones.

Recall the opening line of Elizabeth Bishop's "Brazil, January 1, 1502": "Januaries, Nature greets our eyes." The first thing my ear notices about this line is the diction, which is dull. We're dealing in generalities here—"Januaries, Nature"—not the most typical province of poetic language. The second thing I notice is that the line is a pentameter: "Januaries, Nature greets our eyes." A tone has been established. This poem is speaking calmly and loftily about how things are, seemingly unaware that how things are doesn't sound very interesting.

> Januaries, Nature greets our eyes
> exactly as she must have greeted theirs.

Like anybody who's spent time with this poem, I know that the pronoun *theirs* refers to the Portuguese who first observed the harbor at Rio de Janeiro on January 1, 1502. But every time I hear the opening lines, the pronoun sounds weirdly unspecific, even more so than the noun *Nature*. For while the pronoun wants to point to particular people in a particular place and time, the poem doesn't tell me who or where or when. I'm pushed forward into the linear process of discovery that is the life of the poem, yet for many lines there is little to discover—only the fact that leaves may be large or small, flowers yellow or pink.

At the same time, the versification seems to be getting soggy. The second line is also a pentameter ("ex**act**ly **as** she **must** have **greet**ed **theirs**"), but unlike its predecessor, in which the stressed syllables match the normal intonation of the clause ("**Jan**uaries, **Nat**ure **greets** our **eyes**"), this pentameter asks us to put a heavy stress on the word *as*, a word we wouldn't ordinarily stress. Quickly, any sense of a consistent metric disappears from the poem. What's more, while the opening line is enjambed, asking us to put particular pressure on the word *exactly*, every subsequent line ends either with a full stop or by parsing the syntax—by breaking the syntax in a predictable place rather than using the line endings to energize the syntax.

> big leaves, little leaves, and giant leaves,
> blue, blue-green, and olive.

"Brazil, January 1, 1502" doesn't sound like "The Dry Salvages," but, like Eliot, Bishop has relinquished the power of the most basic poetic devices. Rather than fulfilling the sonic and semantic expectations aroused by its first two lines, "Brazil, January 1, 1502" attenuates that relinquishment for so long that we may cease to be aroused. Why does its opening stanza seem so deeply invested in getting things "exactly" right when there is no apparent reason for getting things right?

Context, once again, is all, and the final stanza of the poem supplies it. In contrast to the lassitude of the poem's opening lines, the diction here is bracingly concrete, the syntax hungry for predication.

> Just so the Christians, hard as nails,
> tiny as nails, and glinting,
> in creaking armor, came and found it all,
> not unfamiliar:
> no lovers' walks, no bowers,
> no cherries to be picked, no lute music,
> but corresponding, nevertheless,
> to an old dream of wealth and luxury
> already out of style when they left home—
> wealth, plus a brand-new pleasure.

When the Portuguese arrived on January 1, 1502, Bishop explains, they were incurious enough to find the new world landscape "not unfamiliar." They presumed the harbor into which they sailed to be the mouth of a great river, which they named Rio de Janeiro—river of January. But there is no river. Error is built into the very name of the place, and once we register how the energetic language in Bishop's poem is presenting a new world landscape as an allegory for old world values ("Still in the foreground there is Sin"), we have to wonder if a similar imposition of values might have been taking place in the low-energy language of the poem's opening: "Januaries, Nature greets our eyes / exactly as she must have greeted theirs." Who said nature was a girl? Is nature feminine in the same way that a flower might be purple, yellow, or pink? Is exactitude opposed to error, or is it a species of error? At the end of the poem, when we see the Portuguese entering their own representation of the foreign landscape—"they ripped away into the hanging fabric, / each out to catch an Indian for himself"—then the poem's opening lines feel not pointlessly lackadaisical but pointedly contrived, a provocation.

That provocation is at once ethical and aesthetic. But while the poem's ethical dilemma feels resolved by the end of the poem, which condemns the Portuguese for their rapaciousness, the aesthetic dilemma remains naggingly unresolved. For no matter how many times we've read "Brazil, January 1, 1502," no matter how clearly we remember that the poem will contextualize its opening lines, those lines also continue to feel flatly pointless, resisting the context that also makes them meaningful. If they didn't do so, if their lassitude didn't last long enough to disrupt our sense of proportion and dissipate our wish for gratification, then the poem would feel like a puzzle we've already solved, a problem we need to think about only once. Instead, the poem asks us to live in time, the time in which we think and breathe, repeating ourselves, correcting ourselves. It asks us to recognize that by living in time we don't simply diagnose error but inhabit it, returning again and again to the beginning with a renewed sense of the inadequacy of our sharpest discriminations.

One of the most thrilling pentameters in Shakespeare is "Kill,

kill, kill, kill, kill him! Hold, hold, hold, hold!" but how could one possibly determine, outside of the scene in *Coriolanus* in which it occurs, that the line is good or bad? How could one even tell that it's a pentameter? These questions rest on a foundational presupposition: the effect of a particular aesthetic gesture is never predictably good or bad or anything in itself; its success depends on its relationship to other effects. Questions of value are more charged when we're trying to describe the crucial presence in art of an effect that in itself seems purposeless—an effect that depends on the abandonment of all our usual tools for describing how and why an artistic medium is worthy of our attention; but the presupposition on which the questions rest remains the same. So while the only plausible answer to the question "Can bad writing be a virtue?" is never, the question needs continually to be raised if works of art are to remain open to the full range of possibilities inherent in their mediums. And it needs to be raised by the works of art themselves, works that invigorate our standards of excellence by confounding given notions of what constitutes them.

The Door Ajar

What makes a human being make a poem? Why does the language we employ every day—language suited equally well to thank-you notes and parking tickets—ask to be liberated from its more workaday chores, its rhythmic vitality threatening to overpower its capacity for plain sense? Why may the lack of vitality feel equally uncanny in its refusal to corroborate plain sense? We don't reread *King Lear* simply because we can't remember the story; we reread because we want to feel our familiar world becoming strange again.

A friend of your brother sends you a gift, a painting of Indian pipes, which is your favorite flower. You write a thank-you note: "I know not how to thank you." Because your brother's wife is your closest friend, you have refused to meet the bearer of the gift: you know, as most people do not, that your brother's friend is in fact his mistress. You know this because their assignations have taken place in your own house, in the dining room, on a black horsehair sofa in front of the fire. The assignations have been facilitated by your sister, with whom you share the house your grandfather built. Your brother, his wife, and their three children live next door in a house your father built for them.

Another gift arrives: a yellow jug painted with red trumpet-vine flowers. You are being wooed by your brother's mistress, but unlike your sister, whose primary allegiance is to your brother, you remain steadfastly devoted to your brother's wife and children, from whom your brother has withdrawn his daily affection; there will be "no treason," you tell the oldest child. To the mistress you write a second note.

> Nature forgot—The Circus reminded her—
> Thanks for the Ethiopian Face.
> The Orient is in the West.
> "You knew, Oh Egypt" said the entangled Antony—

For all intents and purposes, this is a thank-you note, but because its language fails so aggressively to embody those intents and purposes, it feels like a poem. The writer does not mean merely to refer to the occasion at hand, the receipt of a gift, but also to force the giver to attend to a new and more pressing occasion: the reality of the language itself. Does the writer mean to compare the giver to the Ethiopian Queen of Sheba, making herself King Solomon, recipient of the queen's gifts? Does she mean to compare the giver to Shakespeare's luxuriously two-faced Cleopatra? To a circus? The recipient of this thank-you note would be baffled, threatened, or enraged by these provocative metaphors. The reader of this poem would be thrilled—not simply by the metaphors themselves but also with the speed with which one provocation is superseded by another.

Emily Dickinson, infamous recluse, the author of some 1,775 poems, most of which remained unpublished until after her death, is the writer of the thank-you notes. The adulterers are Austin Dickinson, her brother, and Mabel Loomis Todd, who first laid eyes on Dickinson only when she was lying in her coffin but who became the first editor of Dickinson's poems. Austin's spurned wife is Susan Gilbert Dickinson, with whom Dickinson shared 276 of her poems, including many of her greatest.

"With the exception of Shakespeare," wrote Dickinson to Sue, "you have told me of more knowledge than any one living."

Sue would eventually publish the poems in her possession, and her daughter, Mattie, would continue until her death in 1943 to exert her mother's right to do so. Until her death in 1968, Mabel Loomis Todd's daughter, Millicent, would exert her mother's right to do the same thing, a right that was perhaps unintentionally bequeathed to Mabel by Dickinson's sister, Vinnie, who asked Mabel to transcribe the hundreds of poems found in Dickinson's bedroom after her death. Lies, vendettas, and lawsuits proliferated: a drama of marital infidelity was played out over the dead poet's manuscripts with an intricacy that Henry James could not have imagined. The last major player in this drama, Mary Hampson (the second wife of Mattie's companion, Alfred Leete Hampson), died in 1988. Until the end, she lived in the house that Dickinson's father built for Austin and Sue, the Evergreens, and the house has remained basically unchanged since the poet's lifetime. Dickinson last entered the Evergreens on the night of August 4, 1883, when she came to sit beside her dying nephew Gib. Today, Gib's rocking horse still stands in a shroud of dust beside his bed.

When Lyndall Gordon, the most recent of Dickinson's biographers, says that Austin's betrayal of Sue was "the only drama in Dickinson's life that's not of her making," she means to emphasize the fact that Emily Dickinson was an extraordinarily bold woman, an artist who was intimidated by nothing—the opposite of a fear-driven recluse, the opposite of the lovelorn spinster. The people to whom Dickinson was most closely related or most passionately attracted were rampant, larger-than-life figures, and her power dwarfed even theirs. When her brother, Austin, wanted to give his mistress a parcel of Dickinson land, her sister, Vinnie, consented but Emily refused to sign the deed: she controlled that narrative. Her refusal to meet the mistress was similarly no act of reticence but, like her thank-you note, an act of withering aggression. People were scared of Emily Dickinson, and rightly so.

"We do not have much poetry," said the teenaged Dickinson of her household, "father having made up his mind that it's pretty much all *real life*. Father's real life and *mine* sometimes come into collision, but as yet, escape unhurt!" The collision was between the everyday language of thank-you notes and the disruptive language of poetry, of which Dickinson was a native speaker. Once, when her mother was trying to make a houseguest comfortable, Dickinson couldn't help but transform her mother's solicitous questions into provocations: "Wouldn't you like to have the Declaration of Independence to read? Or the Lord's Prayer repeated?" It's hard to imagine how such biting repartee would be received, and neither did Dickinson hold back when the stakes were higher. "Have you said your prayers?" demanded her teacher at Mount Holyoke Female Seminary. "Yes," she answered, "though it can't make much difference to The Creator."

When Dickinson was dealing not with figures of authority but with her peers, people with whom she hoped to share the intensity that distinguished her, the stakes were even higher. "I have dared to do strange things—bold things," she confided to her friend Jane Humphrey, "and have asked no advice from any—I have heeded beautiful tempters, and do not think I am wrong. . . . Oh Jennie, it would relieve me to tell you all, to sit down at your feet, and look in your eyes, and confess what *you only* shall know." Jane Humphrey did not respond to this letter. "No day goes by, little One, but has its thought of you, and its wish to see you," Dickinson wrote to Jane five years later. Again there was no response. It's tempting to speculate about the revelation Dickinson longed to make, but all speculation inevitably feels inadequate. "I have dared to do strange things—bold things": this is the language of poetry, not the language of what Dickinson's father called real life. If Jane could have imagined what Dickinson was talking about, she wouldn't have turned away, and her inability to imagine makes Dickinson's ardor seem all the more threatening.

The young Dickinson was so volatile, so volcanic in her intuitions that she could clear a room. Mental and emotional acuity of that level is frightening because people have no way of explaining its source. It requires no nurturing. It expands not only without the intervention of other people but against the will of the person who possesses it—or is possessed by it. It simply happens. Not many people want to have tea with the Delphic Oracle, however mesmerizing her speech. So by a very early age, Dickinson learned that if she were going to have any friends, she needed to prevaricate. She also learned how little she gained from prevarication. The few people to whom she truly made herself available were able to withstand the onslaught. Sue welcomed it. In contrast, after receiving just a couple of well-aimed gusts, Mabel Loomis Todd was shaken to the root, driven to own the poet who would not countenance her, much as she had been driven to possess the poet's brother.

Dickinson's reclusiveness was not a way of protecting herself from the world but a way of protecting the world from herself. Jane Humphrey was the first in a long list of people whom Dickinson frightened simply by existing, and frightening people became a demoralizing occupation. Even more demoralizing was the effort to speak the language of real life: poetry was Dickinson's native tongue—not a transparent sentence like "I know not how to thank you" but elusive sentences like "I have dared to do strange things" or "Thanks for the Ethiopian Face." By the time she sent that sentence to Mabel Loomis Todd, nominally in thanks for the painted jug, Dickinson knew what she was doing, and she knew that it would work. The language of poetry was not fit for all occasions, since even the slightest release of it into the real world could be explosive.

But what makes Dickinson's poems even more threatening is that they blur the difference between the language of everyday life and the language of poetry, making the apparently transparent language of thank-you notes feel explosive—making our own lives feel explosive.

> I cannot live with You—
> It would be Life—
> And life is over there—
> Behind the Shelf
>
> The Sexton keeps the key to—

The language is not complicated here. Only four of these twenty-three words have more than one syllable, and the syllables are arranged in a meter and rhyme scheme familiar to us from innumerable ballads and hymns.

> I **cannot live** with **You**—
> It **would** be **Life**—

But at the same time, Dickinson's idiosyncratic punctuation keeps those syllables from settling too happily into those familiar forms, and the poem's relationship to those forms is as edgy as its professed relationship to the restricting terms of everyday life: to live with another person, however beloved, is to be a pretty piece of porcelain, locked forever behind the sexton's shelf.

The prospect of dying with the beloved—

> I could not die—with You—
> For One must wait
> To shut the Other's Gaze down

—and the prospect of rising together with the beloved after
death—

> Nor could I rise—with You—
> Because Your Face
> Would put out Jesus'

—are no less swiftly rejected. The apparently small space of
human interaction, the space of "strange things—bold things,"
challenges accepted notions of infinitude, and the poem's final
stanza is both witheringly stern and wildly metaphorical in its
acceptance of human limitation.

> So we must meet apart—
> You there—I—here—
> With just the Door ajar
> That Oceans are—and Prayer—
> And that White Sustenance—
> Despair—

Solitude is not a state merely to be chosen. The space between
any two human beings, however proximate, is as immense as
an ocean, and Dickinson lived and wrote in order to honor that
immensity.

As was often her practice, Dickinson offered multiple variants
for crucial words in this poem, leaving little indication of which
word was to be preferred: the "White Sustenance" of despair
might be a "White exercise" or a "White privilege." Dickinson
couldn't choose between these alternatives, and she doesn't
want us to choose either; the existential dilemma embodied
by the poem cannot be locked up in words too easily. This is
why her poems are so endlessly seductive: deploying the simplest of means, they threaten constantly to exceed themselves,
encroaching on infinitude. The despair of isolation might be a

sustenance, and it might be an exercise, but it is also a privilege, for to pretend that oceans do not separate us is paradoxically to exacerbate our alienation.

One of Dickinson's most famous poems describes a state of psychological disorientation that invokes, among other things, one of the most essential pleasures of poetry—its propensity to turn swiftly against itself, the sound of language luring us through a discontinuity of sense.

> The thought behind, I strove to join
> Unto the thought before—
> But Sequence ravelled out of Sound—
> Like Balls—upon a Floor—

This is the feeling aroused by Dickinson's gnomic thank-you note to Mabel Loomis Todd, but poems like "I cannot live with You" exist to make that feeling seductive: by shirking our everyday notions of usefulness, they allow us to take pleasure in what might, in another circumstance, seem merely unnerving.

"Abyss has no Biographer," wrote Dickinson, and the few people who could bear Dickinson's true company were as unnerved by her boldness as the majority of people who could not. Those few were also the kinds of people who like to read poems, the kinds of people who perhaps also want to make them. Dickinson's father was no such person, but at least in one regard he did come to see his daughter truly: as head of the household, he relieved her of morning duties so that she might begin her reading and writing at 3:00 a.m.

Privacy is crucial for any writer, but Dickinson had the inevitable misfortune, especially after her death, of being surrounded by people for whom the act of writing was not private enough, or for whom the act of privacy took on warped and astonishing forms. No ocean was wide enough. The companion of Dickinson's niece Mattie, Alfred Leete Hampson, didn't want to leave Dickinson's manuscripts in the Evergreens while he traveled to Europe, so every winter he packed up almost a thousand poems and more than two hundred letters in a suitcase and took "Emily" along. It's because of the efforts of such people, however complex their motives, that we are now able to read Dickinson at all, but of the many fascinating characters surrounding the poet, my favorite is Dickinson's cousin Loo Norcross, who enraged Mabel Loomis Todd by refusing to hand over the letters Dickinson had written to her. The indomitable Loo kept the letters with her in a nursing home until she died in 1919; then they were burned. It's impossible not to imagine the poet's approval.

> The Soul selects her own Society—
> Then—shuts the Door—

Infinitude

"Folks expect of the poet to indicate more than the beauty and dignity which always attach to dumb real objects," said Walt Whitman in the 1855 preface to *Leaves of Grass:* "they expect him to indicate the path between reality and their souls."

I want to take this expectation as seriously as did the author of "I cannot live with You." For a moment, I want to forget about the poet's place in social and literary history. I don't want to be distracted by our knowledge of how prominent a poet's spiritual aspirations once were—or how sweetly antiquated those aspirations might seem today. My subject is not simply the poet's claim to indicate a path between reality and the soul: I want to examine the ways in which the material language of poetry, the work of diction and syntax, may actually be said to constitute that path.

Though Whitman seems to me the author of the most rivetingly existential account of infinitude in our language, I want to begin with a less ambitious poem, one that suggests what a path between reality and the soul might look like.

> When I heard the learn'd astronomer,
> When the proofs, the figures, were ranged in columns before me,
> When I was shown the charts and diagrams, to add, divide, and measure them,

> When I sitting heard the astronomer where he lectured
>   with much applause in the lecture-room,
> How soon unaccountable I became tired and sick,
> Till rising and gliding out I wander'd off by myself,
> In the mystical moist night-air, and from time to time,
> Look'd up in perfect silence at the stars.

By opposing the communal practice of learnedness to the private accident of perception, this poem predetermines the reader's act of perception: by the second line ("When the proofs, the figures, were ranged in columns before me"), we know that the astronomer is not to be trusted, despite the fact that the syntax keeps going, despite the fact that the poem concludes with the most readily available sound of culmination—an iambic pentameter line.

Written more than a century later, this poem by Louise Glück depends on all the same oppositions, except that our attitudes toward both scientific learnedness and private perception have been scrambled. "There is a moment after you move your eye away," begins "Telescope," "when you forget where you are."

> You're not a creature in a body.
> You exist as the stars exist,
> participating in their stillness, their immensity.
>
> Then you're in the world again.
> At night, on a cold hill,
> taking the telescope apart.
>
> You realize afterward
> not that the image is false,
> but the relation is false.

> You see again how far away
> each thing is from every other thing.

Here, the astronomer's instrument becomes the means through which we feel wonder—not while we're looking through the telescope but in the moment after we move our eye from its lens. Then the feeling passes, and only at this moment, at the beginning of the poem's seventh sentence, does Glück tell us where we are: on a cold hill, taking the telescope apart. The poem's most basic narrative information is delayed so that we might feel its mere recital as revelation. For the poem's mission is not to assert the incomprehensible distance of the stars, but to make us feel the incomprehensible distance between ourselves and what appears most near to us. In the scrupulous vocabulary of the poem itself, we are not wrong to feel wonder at the "image" of the night sky; but we are wrong to think of our "relation" to the stars as being more inexplicable than our relation to any other thing, no matter how close, no matter how familiar.

"The sentence in which god comes to be involved in words is not 'I believe in god,'" says the philosopher Emmanuel Levinas. "It is the 'here I am,' said to the neighbor to whom I am given over." For Levinas, the infinite is not an ontological category. It is no more inevitably to be found in the night sky than in an astronomy classroom, though it is more likely to be found through the human interaction afforded by places like a classroom: there is no relation more harrowing and more inexplicable than the relation with whatever is plainly in front of our faces. This, as I've suggested, is the shocking revelation of the end of Emily Dickinson's "I cannot live with You."

> So we must meet apart—
> You there—I—here—

With just the Door ajar
That Oceans are—and Prayer—
And that White Sustenance—
Despair—

"To have the idea of infinity it is necessary to exist as separated," says Levinas, as if glossing Dickinson's poem, and this act of separation entails a rejection of any given image of infinitude, the soul, the stars, heaven—call it what you will. To feel at home in the world is to have eradicated the desire for infinitude. To depend on the night sky to kindle that desire is ultimately to squelch it.

In the terms of Glück's "Telescope," the feeling of infinitude is produced not by the image of any particular thing but by the relation between things. The final lines of her poem are also startling ("You see again how far away / each thing is from every other thing") because they reduce the perceiving human mind to the status of mere "thing" while simultaneously suggesting that all such things, no matter how familiar, no matter how close at hand, participate in the mysterious grandeur we associate with infinite space. What's more, the poem does not simply explain these terms to us: it places us in a particular relation to the image it renders, and the act of reading the poem is the process of coming to inhabit that relation. By exceeding itself, the language of the poem participates in the conjuring of infinitude, leading us to conclusions we could not have predicted readily at the beginning of the poem. When this happens in the final lines, a gulf opens, and we feel the unfathomed distance between us and the very thing with which we assumed we were intimate: the poem.

Just how far away is each thing is from every other thing? Here is a list of things from the beginning of Whitman's "As

I Ebb'd with the Ocean of Life," a poem that makes us inhabit distance more witheringly than any poem I know.

> Chaff, straw, splinters of wood, weeds, and the sea-gluten.

Here is a list of things from the end of "As I Ebb'd with the Ocean of Life."

> Tufts of straw, sands, fragments.

The thrill of this poem is that it can appear to have traveled nowhere, ending in the same place, in the same rhetoric, with which it began. But while its images of things remain pretty much the same, our relation to those things has been radically disoriented. In the first line I've quoted, the images refuse to be linked to anything beyond themselves, but in the second line, the images are wildly metaphorical, conjuring a palpable but indeterminate sense of otherness. How does Whitman alter our relation to these images? How does he make us travel this immense distance without ever diverting our eyes from the unchanging ground beneath our feet?

The poem's first section concludes with this sentence.

> Fascinated, my eyes reverting from the south, dropt, to follow those slender windrows,
> Chaff, straw, splinters of wood, weeds, and the sea-gluten,
> Scum, scales from shining rocks, leaves of salt-lettuce, left by the tide,
> Miles walking, the sound of breaking waves the other side of me,
> Paumanok there and then as I thought of the old thought of likenesses,
> These you presented to me you fish-shaped island,

As I wended the shores I know,
As I walk'd with that electric self seeking types.

Here, Whitman refuses the gesture with which he concludes "When I Heard the Learn'd Astronomer": he refuses to look up. Though he wanders the shoreline "seeking types" in a poem that was originally called "Bardic Symbols," he does not look away from the things that so stalwartly refuse to be made meaningful; instead, he feels his immense separation from those things. The idea of infinity requires separation, as both Dickinson and Levinas suggest; but Whitman must inhabit his desolation with an intensity the poem has not yet imagined. He must become a thing himself.

I too but signify at the utmost a little wash'd-up drift,
A few sands and dead leaves to gather,
Gather, and merge myself as part of the sands and drift.

As in the final lines of Glück's "Telescope," in which the perceiving mind becomes a thing among things, this transformation is simultaneously emptying and revelatory. Emptying because Whitman has aligned himself with things that seem completely lacking in interiority; revelatory because the act of entering into this relation with things is itself immensely suggestive. The chaff, straw, splinters, and weeds are like nothing, but Whitman is like them. How does it feel to be like something that is like nothing? It feels, answers the poem, as if the self were divided, unlike itself.

O baffled, balk'd, bent to the very earth,
Oppress'd with myself that I have dared to open my
mouth,
Aware now that amid all that blab whose echoes recoil
upon me

> I have not once had the least idea who or what I am,
> But that before all my arrogant poems the real ME stands
>   yet untouch'd, untold, altogether unreach'd,
> Withdrawn far, mocking me with mock-congratulatory
>   signs and bows,
> With peals of distant ironical laughter at every word I
>   have written,
> Pointing in silence to these songs, and then to the sand
>   beneath.
>
> I perceive I have not really understood any thing, not a
>   single object, and that no man ever can.

At this extraordinary midpoint in the poem, Whitman is bent to the earth, locked to the sand beneath his feet, and the act of averting his eyes to the stars—or to any other image of spiritual plenitude—is literally unimaginable. While Whitman looks at the earth, the "real ME" looks at him, pointing first to the poems and then to the sand. The gesture equates them, suggesting that they are both things, equally bereft of meaningfulness. This refusal of likeness is once again based on an assertion of likeness: the sand is like nothing and the poems are like the sand. But if there is consolation to be had in this complexity, Whitman refuses it as well. His most astonishing gestures are always simple to the point of flatness, and "I perceive I have not really understood any thing, not a single object, and that no man ever can" is the most astonishing line he ever wrote. The line is no pentameter, it does not sing, it has no tone. It is adamant, repetitive, and it does not feel like hyperbole.

> I perceive I have not really understood any thing, not a
>   single object, and that no man ever can.

How does a poem recover from such a line? How does poetry recover from such a line?

"I hold you so firm till you answer me something," says Whitman to the barren earth. Like Glück, he is confronting the immense distance between himself and the other: this is where "Telescope" ends, with the stark inhabitation of a relation. But unlike Glück, Whitman moves on from insight to rage, refusing to accept the relation. This effort is doomed, however: the earth will not speak to him, and rage must be superseded by submission. Whitman must speak for himself among others, and it is this final act of speaking, of exceeding the given terms of the poem, that constitutes the irruption of infinitude. This happens not in spite of the fact that Whitman has become a body in the most desolate sense; it happens because he inhabits that condition utterly, speaking from it.

The poem concludes with this sentence.

> Me and mine, loose windrows, little corpses,
> Froth, snowy white, and bubbles,
> (See, from my dead lips the ooze exuding at last,
> See, the prismatic colors of glistening and rolling,)
> Tufts of straw, sands, fragments,
> Buoy'd hither from many moods, one contradicting
>   another,
> From the storm, the long calm, the darkness, the swell,
> Musing, pondering, a breath, a briny tear, dab of liquid
>   or soil,
> Up just as much out of fathomless workings fermented
>   and thrown,
> A limp blossom or two, torn, just as much over waves
>   floating, drifted at random,
> Just as much for us that sobbing dirge of nature,

> Just as much whence we come that blare of the
>   cloud-trumpets,
> We, capricious, brought hither we know not whence,
>   spread out before you,
> You up there walking or sitting,
> Whoever you are, we too lie in drifts at your feet.

The predicate of this sentence is delayed until the final line: we lie. Preceding the subject of the sentence are appositions to the subject—all the things of the world with which Whitman claims kinship: tufts of straw, sand, fragments. Like those things, Whitman himself is a dead thing; he has been buoy'd, fermented, thrown, torn. Even the fantasy of the earth's voice has been abandoned. Speaking out of this deprivation, not against it, Whitman begins a sentence with the word *me*, ending the sentence with a *we* that addresses a *you*. He has not turned his face from the ground beneath him, but the "you" is above him, looking down on him as he looks down at the ground.

We don't know who the "you" is, and efforts to identify it clearly seem to me beside the point. For although Whitman has gestured obscurely to "this phantom" in lines preceding the poem's final fifteen-line sentence, the phantom does not exist meaningfully until Whitman utters the word *you* in the thirteenth line: "We, capricious, brought hither we know not whence, spread out before you." By inhabiting his relation with the things below him so utterly, Whitman is gripped by the sense of something above him, something beyond him, something that looks at him as he looks at the images spread before him. When this happens, and it happens in the movement of syntax, all the dead things of the world are suddenly alive in their relation with the mysterious other who countenances them. Everything—even Whitman himself, speaker of the sentence, beholder of things—becomes a metaphor for something else: "Whoever you are, we too lie in drifts at your feet."

"As I Ebb'd with the Ocean of Life" is often discussed as if it were its author's farewell to poetic inspiration, and the contexts of both literary and social history might support the assertion. Whitman first collected the poem in the 1860 edition of *Leaves of Grass*, where it follows pointedly on *Chants Democratic and Native American*, his response to the political crisis of American democracy. But even if "As I Ebb'd with the Ocean of Life" came to Whitman at the end of something, the poem does not describe the end of poetry. Instead, it describes the relation from which the greatest poetry has always sprung—a separation so acute, an ocean so wide, that the discovery of intimacy with dumb real objects becomes the source of an overwhelming sense of infinitude. The poem not only describes this relation but also enacts it, making the poem itself the process through which the possibility of infinitude is spoken.

So while the early exuberance of "Song of Myself" or "Crossing Brooklyn Ferry" may seem immune to the realization that "I have not really understood any thing," Whitman is (like Yeats at his strongest) unseduced by his own most charismatic thinking. In "Crossing Brooklyn Ferry" he explicitly denies the great distance between all things ("distance avails not"), but his unrelenting catalog of the multitudes contained within him undermines the denial: the force of syntactical repetition threatens to degenerate from rapture to routine, and it's not surprising that Whitman quickly finds himself admitting that "the best I had done seem'd to me blank and suspicious." The sustained texture of the even more extraordinarily attenuated "Song of Myself" depends on these self-interrogating flights of linguistic power.

So does the texture of lyric poems like Glück's "Telescope"— the language constitutes the poem's relationship to the possibility of infinitude. Yet we tend to call a poem like "Telescope" restrained while we reserve the word *excessive* for poems like Whitman's. And however restrained or excessive any poem may seem, we can always imagine poems that are more restrained or more excessive, just as we can point to poems that seem more compressed or more dilated, more anchored in particularity or more conversant with infinitude. Whitman's "As I Ebb'd with the Ocean of Life" partakes simultaneously of all of these qualities, but the poem is not in this regard exceptional; admirers of lyrics like "Telescope," "The Sick Rose," or "Fan-Piece, for Her Imperial Lord" are not at liberty to imagine that *Leaves of Grass, Jerusalem,* or *The Pisan Cantos* are simply in need of a strict editor. These poems transform what might otherwise be egregious excess into a necessity, but it is an often baffling necessity, one that challenges us to confront the way in which excess is central to the making of any work of art, no matter how small.

A Fine Excess

O n May 3, 1945, two years after a federal grand jury in-
dicted him for treason, Ezra Pound was taken prisoner
by Italian partisans and handed over to the United States
Counter Intelligence Corps in Genoa. Several weeks later,
he was transferred to the U.S. Army's Disciplinary Training
Center near Pisa, where he was held first in a steel cage and
later in a tent in the medical compound. Here, on a yellow
pad turned sideways, Pound began writing *The Pisan Cantos*,
the first and longest of which leaps between descriptions of
the center, remarks about contemporary politics, observations
of the natural world, and memories of Pound's youth. The
poem feels driven, unrelentingly purposeful, but at the same
time chaotic, driven by forces beyond the will. Any immediate
evidence of structure, any sense of direction on which readers
might model their own, is buried under the sheer onslaught of
material. "Perhaps one thing we shouldn't lose sight of," says
the psychologist Adam Phillips, "is just how reassuring the
whole idea of excess can be."

Is this poem excessive or restrained?

> O Rose, thou art sick.
> The invisible worm,
> That flies in the night
> In the howling storm:

> Has found out thy bed
> Of crimson joy:
> And his dark secret love
> Does thy life destroy.

These thirty-four words contain forty-one syllables, and, like every poet I've discussed, Blake wants us to experience the linear unfolding of these syllables in a particular way: every line of "The Sick Rose" contains two stressed syllables.

> The in**vis**ible **worm,**
> That **flies** in the **night**
> In the **howl**ing **storm**

Sometimes two unstressed syllables intervene between the stressed syllables ("**flies** in the **night**"), sometimes only one ("**howl**ing **storm**"). And sometimes the line is made exclusively of Germanic monosyllables ("**Rose**, thou art **sick**") while at other times the line includes a multisyllabic Latinate word ("in**vis**ible **worm**"), making the intervening unstressed syllables move more quickly, less punchily. The anapest "thou art **sick**" sounds completely different from the anapest "-ible **worm**."

This elegant dance of pattern and variation becomes itself a kind of pattern; we expect to keep hearing it. But at the end of the poem Blake disrupts our expectations. Each of the final three lines features a disyllabic Latinate word paired with a Germanic monosyllable ("crimson joy," "secret love," "life destroy"), and because our ears are so used to hearing the lilting intervention of unstressed syllables between the stresses—

> Has **found** out thy **bed**
> Of **crim**son **joy**

—our ears want to hear the next lines this way:

And his **dark** secret **love**
Does thy **life** des**troy.**

But we can't hear the lines that way. Because the first syllable of
the word *secret* receives more stress than the second ("**se**cret"),
its long vowel sound preceded by a cluster of mouth-filling consonants, a third stressed syllable has muscled its way into the
line and plunked itself down beside another stressed syllable—
no intervening unstressed syllables, no lilt.

And his **dark se**cret **love**
Does thy **life** des**troy.**

To hear this violation of the pattern, the two stressed syllables
placed violently side by side ("**dark se**cret **love**"), is to know that
no matter what "The Sick Rose" seems to say about that nasty
worm destroying the pretty rose, Blake is completely in favor of
dark secret love. For the poem doesn't simply describe this at-
traction to the dark, the disruptive, the demonic; the sound of
the syllables makes us feel it. And then we want to feel it again.

"The road of excess leads to the palace of wisdom," said
Blake in "The Marriage of Heaven and Hell." Does the metrical
variation in the penultimate line of "The Sick Rose" represent a
moment of excess (from *excedere,* to go beyond) or a moment
of restraint (from *restringere,* to draw back)? As I mentioned at
the beginning of this book, restraint may seem merely banal,
an unexamined trust of limitation, and excess may seem obvious, an unexamined romance with transgression—except inasmuch as a particular work of art creates the context in which
a particular aesthetic choice becomes a virtue. Blake's poem
enacts this paradoxical economy through sublimely ordinary
means: a variation from an established pattern of stressed and
unstressed syllables.

The Pisan Cantos enacts this economy not only on the microscopic level of prosody but also in the grandest terms of structure, simultaneously establishing and obliterating the context in which transgression becomes meaningful. Throughout Canto 74, the first of *The Pisan Cantos*, Pound offers a variety of metaphors for the poem's wayward accumulation of detail. He dismisses general concepts that "cannot be born from a sufficient phalanx of particulars," suggesting that the task of his poem is to provide such a phalanx. "By no means an orderly Dantescan rising / but as the winds veer," he admonishes, suggesting that the phalanx of particulars cannot be organized by the hierarchies familiar to us from centuries of Western thought. "As the winds veer in periplum," he elaborates, associating our readerly voyage not with the bird's-eye perspective of a conventional map but with the periplum, the shipboard view of how the shoreline appears as it is encountered incrementally in time. Neither should we mourn the loss of any centralized perspective. "Le Paradis n'est pas artificiel," he intones, recalling Baudelaire: whatever we know of paradise we know from the disjointed world of particularity itself—"it exists only in fragments unexpected excellent sausage, / the smell of mint, for example."

All these metaphors are reassuring, since they suggest that we're supposed to feel disoriented as we move forward through the poem, overwhelmed by the unruly accumulation of particulars. They suggest that the poem's waywardness is not simply a reflection of the chaotic conditions under which it was written but also the embodiment of a concertedly antihierarchical worldview. But the longer we read, the more dissatisfying these metaphors become. They justify the poem's highly disjunctive texture, but they don't help us actually to negotiate that texture. Many other poems are far longer than Canto 74 (Whitman's "Song of Myself" is almost twice as long), but the length of

Canto 74 feels dauntingly excessive because the poem's material exceeds the grasp of its gathering metaphors. The metaphors urge us to enjoy the fragmented multiplicity of human experience, but instead we feel uneasy, disoriented—as we'd feel in "The Sick Rose" if every line contained the kind of highly charged metrical variation that distinguishes its conclusion. In such a poem, variation no longer feels disruptive; over time, readers become inattentive to the very thing that most demands their attention.

Pound suspects that his readers will feel this way.

> I don't know how humanity stands it
> with a painted paradise at the end of it
> without a painted paradise at the end of it
> the dwarf morning-glory twines round the grass blade

Faced with an indigestible glut of information, readers may find the lack of any organizing teleology ("without a painted paradise at the end") as oppressive as the overbearing force of teleology ("with a painted paradise at the end"), and they are left only with one of the poem's nearly infinite array of meticulously rendered particulars: "the dwarf morning-glory twines round the grass blade." As it is for Whitman, the up-close concentration on things of this world is at once revelatory and emptying, the simultaneous discovery of infinity and mortality.

Pound never relaxed in his devotion to poetic compression, and in contrast to the dilated passages in Eliot's *Four Quartets*, *The Pisan Cantos* is distinguished everywhere by an unrelenting density of language. It's hard not to hear the majority of the eleven syllables in this line as stressed syllables: "the **dwarf morn**ing-**glory twines round** the **grass blade**." Subsequent lines add an even greater semantic charge to this sonic density by juxtaposing a phrase in Latin ("great night of the soul") with references to the Crucifixion, the middle passage, and a litany of the names of fellow prisoners in the Disciplinary Training Center. The phalanx of particulars accumulates with a disorienting swiftness.

> The dwarf morning-glory twines round the grass blade
> magna NOX animae   with Barabbas and 2 thieves
>   beside me,
>   the wards like a slave ship,
>   Mr Edwards, Hudson, Henry

Any reader might be forgiven for giving up at this point, since almost every line of Canto 74 demands a meticulous attention, diverting its readers from the increasingly unmanageable task of seeing the poem whole.

But if we turn to Canto 75, the second and shortest of *The Pisan Cantos*, we find something different. Following the 842 lines of Canto 74, this canto contains just 7 lines of verse followed by 124 measures of a musical score, written out by hand. The score is a twentieth-century transcription for violin of Francesco da Milano's sixteenth-century transcription for lute of Clément Janequin's "Song of the Birds," a polyphonic motet for four voices. The score reduces the multiple voices of polyphony to a single voice, replacing sung syllables with pure sound, while simultaneously offering a visual equivalent of an experience that (as we find out later in *The Pisan Cantos*) Pound had every day he was incarcerated.

> 8th day of September
>   f   f
>   d
>   g
>   write the birds on their treble scale

Magpies, their downy white chests rimmed in black, continually repositioned themselves on the wires surrounding the Disciplinary Training Center, as if to create the musical score of their own singing. This image is seductive: following the cacophonous multiplicity of Canto 74, it answers our desire for lyric singularity—the song is what it means. But to say that Pound aspired to the immediacy of birdsong in *The Pisan Cantos* does not do our experience of the poem justice, since Pound is not suggesting that he would compose a well-made lyric if only he could. "The Sick Rose" may seem restrained compared to *The Pisan Cantos*, but it is excessive in relationship to itself.

This discomfort with the parameters of the lyric is essential to the lyric, and Pound is by no means the only poet to feel it.

> The vastest earthly Day
> Is shrunken small
> By one Defaulting Face
> Behind a Pall—

This poem by Emily Dickinson sets life against death, vastness against smallness, infinitude against finitude: the death of even one person reduces the earth. But Dickinson was not content with piety, even though most reading editions of her poems might suggest in this case that she was. As I've mentioned, Dickinson often offered several choices for certain words in her poems: the "vastest earthly Day" might be "shrunken" small, but it might also be "shriveled" or "dwindled." More provocatively, it might be "chastened." To imagine that the earth is "chastened small" by "one Defaulting Face" is to grant that small face an astonishing agency, and Dickinson recognizes the astonishment by wondering if the face should be not "defaulting" but "heroic," larger than life or death.

> The vastest earthly Day
> Is chastened small
> By one heroic Face
> that owned it all—

This version of the poem is no more authoritative than the one I quoted earlier. Like Pound, Dickinson is of two minds about a singular poetic voice, and the versions of her poem that I've constructed from her variants make choices that Dickinson herself declined to make: the first version laments the finitude of every human being, however insignificant, and the second version insists that an extraordinary human being may exceed her finitude, chastening the earth. But while the poem is anxious not to choose between these alternatives, preferring to equivocate, this anxiety itself suggests a preference for an imagination that wants to *own it all*. The poem is discontent with its own parameters, and Dickinson's refusal of the limitations of conventional publication allowed her to preserve this desire to exceed herself.

Because all poems are formal mechanisms, forged from the limited resources of the language, all poems are bound up in this dilemma: like the mortal beings who make them, poems want to exceed the restraints without which they could never have existed in the first place. But not all poems embody this dilemma as aggressively as *The Pisan Cantos* does. Years before he knew he was sick, Keats expressed "fears that I may cease to be / Before my pen has glean'd my teeming brain," and throughout *The Pisan Cantos* the space of the teeming brain is figured as a six-foot-by-six-foot steel cage. Pound had nothing from which to make his poem except the contents of his own mind—memories, opinions, regrets, dreams—and he feared he was losing his mind. In a sense, this is all the material any poet ever has, and if Pound's situation feels poignant, it is because the situation so viciously literalizes the precariousness of any act of imaginative creation. The poem's excess, like any poem's excess, is driven by the wish not to die; but because the wish is experienced in such a primal form, the poem dramatizes its romance with excess excessively. Like any human being, but unlike most poems, *The Pisan Cantos* asks for more than it deserves.

This is why a satisfying reading of Canto 74 may neither turn away from the poem's unmanageable excess nor pretend to have encompassed it. We may neither ignore Pound's gathering metaphors nor pretend that they account fully for his need to set down on the page everything he sees, thinks, and remembers. Pound first began to organize longer poems through the juxtaposition of tones in the early "Villanelle: The Psychological Hour," as we've seen, and throughout Canto 74 he lurches wildly among a variety of radically different tones, from harangues about contemporary politics and economics on the one hand—

> and in India the rate down to 18 per hundred
> but the local loan lice provided from imported bankers
> so the total interest sweated out of the Indian farmers
> rose in Churchillian grandeur

—to reverent observations of the natural world on the other.

> and there was a smell of mint under the tent flaps
> especially after the rain
> and a white ox on the road toward Pisa
> as if facing the tower,
> dark sheep in the drill field and on wet days were clouds
> in the mountain as if under the guard roosts.
> A lizard upheld me
> the wild birds wd not eat the white bread

> from Mt Taishan to the sunset
> From Carrara stone to the tower
> and this day the air was made open
> for Kuanon of all delights
> Linus, Cletus, Clement

Some of these passages are immediately explicable and some are not, and even the most transparently lyrical passages are larger, more far-reaching than they seem. Our sense of Pound's heterogeneous spiritualism, rising from his reverence for the natural world, is sharpened once we know that Taishan is a sacred mountain in China, that Kuanon is the Japanese name for the Chinese goddess of mercy, and that Linus, Cletus, and Clement are Roman church fathers. But is our reading of the poem at large assisted by the knowledge that in 1925 Winston Churchill, acting as chancellor of the exchequer, returned British currency to the gold standard, reducing the value of one hundred Indian rupees to eighteen pence? The life of *The Pisan Cantos* inheres not in any of these discrete moments as such but in the way in which the poem twists and turns from one moment to another, fastening to the page the work of a mind desperate to compose itself out of nothing. "Enough is so vast a sweetness," said Dickinson, "I suppose it never occurs." And when a poem is driven by the desperate wish to exceed the boundaries of human mortality, then too much can never be enough.

Still, it's one thing to find oneself sympathizing with Keats on his deathbed and another to find oneself sympathizing with a fascist anti-Semite in a cage. This is why *The Pisan Cantos* must also try our sympathy by resisting all conclusions, churning up more clutter than a mind could possibly deploy. And when the poem does rise to moments of lyric clarity, pure birdsong, it is crucial that we feel not simply their isolated power. Which is more excessive, more arrogant, the lyric moments or the chaotic effusions of language that overwhelm them? Poems as unmanageable as *The Pisan Cantos* ask us to ponder such questions, but so do poems as composed as "The vastest earthly Day"—not because these poems are in different ways about the wish to transcend the limitations of human finitude but because they are made of language.

Consider some language from "The French Revolution," one of the first poems Blake wrote in a version of the long, seven-stress line that would distinguish his unwieldy prophetic works, *Milton* and *Jerusalem*. One of the architects of the revolution, the Abbé de Sièyes, is describing how the rising voice of the people will liberate every immortal soul from the shackles of heaven, and the sentence is a contest of verbs: against the forces that would seal, close, bind, enslave, and depress stands a new force that would break, swell, raise, and expand.

> When the heavens were seal'd with a stone, and the terrible
>   sun clos'd in an orb, and the moon
> Rent from the nations, and each star appointed for watch-
>   ers of night,
> The millions of spirits immortal were bound in the ruins of
>   sulphur heaven
> To wander inslav'd; black, deprest in dark ignorance, kept
>   in awe with the whip,
> To worship terrors, bred from the blood of revenge and
>   breath of desire,
> In beastial forms; or more terrible men, till the dawn of our
>   peaceful morning,
> Till dawn, till morning, till the breaking of clouds, and
>   swelling of winds, and the universal voice,

> Till man raise his darken'd limbs out of the caves of night,
>   his eyes and his heart
> Expand.

Because Blake's ears were so used to hearing the syntax of English poetry organized in lines of five stresses ("to break the pentameter, that was the first heave," said Pound in Canto 81), the seven-stress line felt like a strategic excess, a refusal of restraint that's meant to embody the revolutionary fervor the poem also describes: "The **mill**ions of **spir**its im**mor**tal were **bound** in the **ru**ins of **sul**phur **heav**en."

But after we're accustomed to the sound of the long line, Blake exceeds the terms of his own excess, making it feel in the context of this particular poem like a restraint, just as the two-stress line feels like a restraint in "The Sick Rose." This especially long line sounds like it contains seven stressed syllables only because it exists in the context of other seven-stress lines—

> Till man raise his darken'd limbs out of the caves of night,
>   his eyes and his heart

—and the dramatic enjambment with which it concludes delivers us to the most important verb in the sentence.

> Expand.

The syntax of this statement is very plain, boldly declarative ("his eyes and his heart / Expand"), but we feel its wild force because the statement is delivered to us by a long complex sentence in which the independent clause is preceded by a sequence of dependent clauses ("when the heavens were seal'd," "the terrible sun clos'd," "the moon / Rent") that conspire with the line length in order to throw enormous weight on the concluding verb.

> Expand.

We experience this sentence as expansion, as excess, because it is so rigorously curtailed by patterns of repetition—rhythmic patterns, syntactical patterns, rhetorical patterns.

In a short lyric poem by Blake, Dickinson, or Pound, whether we call the poem formal or free, we tend to hear those patterns immediately, and part of Pound's mission in *The Pisan Cantos* is to deny us any immediate recourse to such patterns, asking us to live in the long and often frustrating task of discovering them—and then rediscovering them after they've been swept away. Blake's long poems stand somewhere between these two extremes. But in any case the act of discovering patterns in art never happens instantaneously; it happens over time, even if the time lapse is very small. In that lapse, we feel excess consorting strenuously with restraint. And if the lapse is very large, we tend to call the poem excessive, and if it is small, we tend to call the poem restrained.

Keats once remarked that poems should surprise us with a "fine excess," a formulation that juxtaposes two Latinate words: *fine* (from *finis*, the end or limit) and *excess* (from *excedere*, to go beyond the limit). The formulation is boldly paradoxical—a limited limitlessness, a finite infinitude, a mortal immortality—but it is also accurate. For whatever else it is, the poem is the words on the page, and its drama of excessiveness is played out within the circumscribed arena of the linguistic medium, over which the poet has complete control. Chaos, like order, is in art a concertedly crafted illusion. So if, like the human beings who make them, poems want to exceed the restraints without which they could never have existed in the first place, then actually to exceed those limitations is to cease to exist. A poem cannot be excessive if is it not also fine.

Correct Catastrophe

W hat do you think the responsibilities of writers in general are when and if war comes," Wallace Stevens was asked on the eve of World War II. "A war is a military state of affairs," he responded, "not a literary one." What did he mean? Would Pound, who eulogized a time "before the world was given over to wars," have agreed? Would Blake or Whitman have doubted a poet's capacity to speak to large-scale public events?

In the fall of 1936, the oldest political weekly in the United States sponsored a poetry prize. Of the 1,800 poems submitted, said the editors of the *Nation*, "the overwhelming majority was concerned with contemporary social conflicts either at home or abroad." The winning poem, Wallace Stevens's "The Men That Are Falling," was an elegy for soldiers recently killed in the Spanish Civil War.

> Taste of the blood upon his martyred lips,
> O pensioners, O demagogues and pay-men!
>
> This death was his belief though death is a stone.
> This man loved earth, not heaven, enough to die.

These lines stand among the most uncharacteristic that Stevens ever published. It's difficult to imagine that the author of a quietly unnerving pentameter like "The river that flows nowhere, like a sea" could have written a highly declamatory line like "Taste of the blood upon his martyred lips."

Yet to read "The Men That Are Falling" beside some of the greatest lyric poems of the twentieth century—"The Snow Man," "A Postcard from the Volcano," "The River of Rivers in Connecticut"—is to be forced to rethink not only the complex terms of Stevens's achievement but also the relationship of poetry to public events at large. Stevens stands simultaneously among the most worldly and the most otherworldly of American poets, and it is paradoxically through his otherworldliness that his respect for the actual world is registered most profoundly. What is uncharacteristic about "The Men That Are Falling" is not the desire to write about a controversial war; Stevens often did that. What distinguishes the poem is the unconvincingly urgent rhetoric in which that desire is registered.

After attending law school, Stevens began working in the insurance industry in 1908. He quickly became one of the country's foremost experts in surety law, and in 1934 he was named vice president of the Hartford Accident and Indemnity Company. "The truth is that we may well be entering an insurance era," he wrote in "Insurance and Social Change," published in 1937, the year in which the first Social Security benefits were paid. Surveying the nationalized insurance schemes of Italy, Germany, and Great Britain, Stevens tried to convince his colleagues that the Social Security Administration posed no threat either to their business or to their personal lives.

Other great modern American poets had full-time jobs. Marianne Moore was an editor, William Carlos Williams was a doctor, T. S. Eliot was a banker and an editor. What distinguishes Stevens is that he never gave the impression of feeling any tension between the different aspects of his life. Once he quipped that "money is a kind of poetry," but more often he emphasized that his legal work was in no way poetic, just as his poems were not meaningfully involved with the logics of law or economics. In an essay called "Surety and Fidelity Claims" he even admitted that his work would seem to almost anyone tedious: "You sign a lot of drafts. You see surprisingly few people. You do the greater part of your work either in your own office or in lawyers' offices." Stevens took that work so seriously that after publishing his first book, *Harmonium*, in 1923, he stopped writing poems for a decade. His daughter Holly was born. "My job is not now with poets from Paris," he told Williams, who was a close friend. "It is to keep the fire-place burning and the music-box churning and the wheels of the baby's chariot turning."

Anyone who cared about American poetry presumed that Stevens's career as a poet was finished, but then "The Idea of Order at Key West" appeared suddenly in 1934. Beginning at the age of fifty-five, Stevens finally assumed the profile of a poet, and the great books of his maturity (*Ideas of Order, The Man with the Blue Guitar, Parts of a World, Transport to Summer,* and *The Auroras of Autumn*) were published at regular intervals. He continued working at the Hartford until well after the age of mandatory retirement; he declined an invitation to be the Charles Eliot Norton Professor of Poetry at Harvard. Shortly before his death in 1955, his *Collected Poems* received both the National Book Award and the Pulitzer Prize.

One of his last poems was "The River of Rivers in Connecticut." "On its banks," says Stevens,

> No shadow walks. The river is fateful,
> Like the last one. But there is no ferryman.
> He could not bend against its propelling force.
>
> It is not to be seen beneath the appearances
> That tell of it. The steeple at Farmington
> Stands glistening and Haddam shines and sways.

> It is the third commonness with light and air,
> A curriculum, a vigor, a local abstraction . . .
> Call it, once more, a river, an unnamed flowing,
>
> Space-filled, reflecting the seasons, the folk-lore
> Of each of the senses; call it, again and again,
> The river that flows nowhere, like a sea.

The river of rivers feels mythic, as momentous as the river that separates us from the afterlife. But this decidedly earthly river is not crossed only once; we need no ferryman, no Charon, to carry us over. The river is fateful because every moment of human life is fateful. It flows through the familiar Connecticut towns of Haddam and Farmington, its water flashes in the sun. It is an emblem of our mortality, an endless flowing, but more importantly it embodies a sweet acceptance of oblivion: the river carries us nowhere, not like the sea, but like a sea— like any sea at all.

Stevens once remarked that while we possess the great poems of heaven and hell, the great poems of the earth remain to be written. Both "The River of Rivers in Connecticut" and "The Men That Are Falling" are products of Stevens's lifelong ambition to write those poems, poems that honor mortality. But even as "The Men That Are Falling" disdains the extremities of heaven and hell, it embraces earth in a language of fitful extremity. In contrast, the consolation of "The River of Rivers in Connecticut" feels enticingly complex because the poem's diction is so eerily generalized, its syntax so quietly declarative. Small things seem magical without ceasing to be themselves. Like Marvell and Yeats (whose magic I've already discussed), Stevens in his most characteristic poems harnesses a plainspoken diction that points beyond the world it also denotes.

Stevens did not take that world for granted, and neither was he capable (as "The Men That Are Falling" suggests) of sustaining his typically hushed tone with equanimity.

> The pressure of the contemporaneous from the time
> of the beginning of the World War to the present
> time has been constant and extreme. No one can
> have lived apart in a happy oblivion.

Stevens made this remark in 1936, in the midst of the Depression, and its insight feels relevant today. Who can have lived apart in a happy oblivion at any moment in the past seventy-five years? Stevens felt no respite from social pressures during the supposedly carefree twenties that followed the First World War, and what Robert Lowell would later call, with exquisite weariness, the unstoppable cycle of "small war on the heels of small / war" has continued to this day. Following September 11 and, subsequently, following the most recent war in Iraq, people who weren't ordinarily interested in poetry turned to poems. Poets who didn't ordinarily pay attention to public events wrote poems responding to them. It's easy to welcome anything that increases the audience of an ancient art, but that welcome may disguise intractable questions. What is a desire to read poetry in a time of social crisis a desire for? Should a poet feel that by writing a poem he has truly fulfilled a social responsibility? Should a reader feel that a poem responding to war is a better poem than a poem about shop windows? That a poem decrying the "taste of blood upon his martyred lips" is better than a poem whispering that the river "flows nowhere, like a sea"?

Consider the familiar opening lines of W. B. Yeats's "The Lake Isle of Innisfree."

> I will arise and go now, and go to Innisfree,
> And a small cabin build there, of clay and wattles made:

> Nine bean-rows will I have there, a hive for the honey-bee,
> And live alone in the bee-loud glade.

These lines, as the poet Louis MacNeice once reminded us, were "inspired by the sight of a London shop window where a little ball was dancing on a jet of water. A poet like W. H. Auden," MacNeice continued, "would most probably have included the little ball in the first verse of the poem, which would not necessarily have been either better or worse for it but which would have become a different poem."

MacNeice's point is that Yeats's poem is no better or worse for having elided the terms of its occasion; speaking as Auden's friend, he didn't want automatically to prefer poems that refer openly to gasworks and wars. Still, it's one thing to notice that a poem might have contained a London shop window but does not. What if the occasion of the poem is a soldier lying dead in his blood? What if a poem elided that occasion? Would that poem be, as MacNeice said, neither better nor worse but merely different from a poem that confronts us with the bodily cost of war?

Consider "The Death of a Soldier," one of the earliest poems in which Stevens achieves the hushed tone that distinguishes his greatest work. "The soldier falls," says Stevens in the first stanza as plainly as possible; ways of making that statement meaningful are then considered in turn.

> He does not become a three-days personage,
> Imposing his separation,
> Calling for pomp.
>
> Death is absolute and without memorial,
> As in a season of autumn,
> When the wind stops,

> When the wind stops and, over the heavens,
> The clouds go, nevertheless,
> In their direction.

Evident here are the preoccupations that distinguish the poems of *Harmonium*, a book whose power does not depend on our feeling the engagement of its poems with the world that provoked them; a book, to put it more coarsely, unlike *The Waste Land* or *A Draft of XVI Cantos*, which were published around the same time. In contrast to the aggressively registered worldliness of Eliot and Pound, "The Death of a Soldier" offers a more generalized philosophical interest in the relationship of human life and natural processes, and, as in the better-known "Snow Man," Stevens is stern in his rejection of narratives of religious or natural consolation: the soldier is not a figure for the risen Christ (no "three-days personage") and neither do the cycles of the natural world stop to record his death; the clouds go nevertheless in their direction, which can't be specified, because it's theirs, not ours. The soldier feels simultaneously worldly and otherworldly, and so does the poem's diction, as if the poem's events were taking place (like the events of "The River of Rivers in Connecticut") simultaneously around the corner and beyond the horizon.

In what way, then, could the poem embody Stevens's sure sense that, since the advent of the First World War, "no one can have lived apart in a happy oblivion"? Because of its tone, "The Death of a Soldier" slips easily into *Harmonium*, but the poem began its life as part of a sequence called "Lettres d'un Soldat," a sequence inspired by the letters of Eugène Lemercier, a French soldier who was killed in the First World War. Originally, the poem was preceded by an epigraph culled from these letters (*"The death of a soldier is close to natural things"*), and the poem exposes the sentimentality of this remark, a sentimentality that may disguise the real horror of useless death by attempting too quickly to make it meaningful.

This is how Stevens's poems most often work: they elaborate the thought provoked by the poem's occasion rather than recording the occasion itself. But once we become aware of the wartime context of his early poems, does our knowledge make *Harmonium* a better book? A worse book? Stevens's poems do not simply provoke such questions; they were themselves animated by such questions, and their diction—the highly deflected relationship of that diction to what Stevens called "the pressure of the contemporaneous"—represents a complex response to such questions. The poet who seems to write in a happy oblivion, removed from that pressure, courts one danger: the danger of seeming aloof, as if communal suffering were for other people. But the poet who covets that pressure, who craves the glamour of catastrophe, courts another danger: the danger of narcissism, of assuming one can speak for a community that has suffered as one has not.

Worse, such a poet may seem cheered up by suffering.

> He was at Naples writing letters home
> And, between his letters, reading paragraphs
> On the sublime. Vesuvius had groaned
> For a month. It was pleasant to be sitting there,
> While the sultriest fulgurations, flickering,
> Cast corners in the glass. He could describe
> The terror of the sound because the sound
> Was ancient. He tried to remember the phrases: pain
> Audible at noon, pain torturing itself,
> Pain killing pain on the very point of pain.
> The volcano trembled in another ether,

As the body trembles at the end of life.

It was almost time for lunch. Pain is human.
There were roses in the cool café. His book
Made sure of the most correct catastrophe.

These opening lines of Stevens's "Esthétique du Mal," written during the Second World War, present a cautionary portrait of the sort of poet I've just described, the poet who has learned too readily to encompass catastrophe. Typically, Stevens does not write openly of the war to which he is responding; he distances himself from the poem's occasion, using the erupting Vesuvius as a figure for catastrophe. And in this sense, the poem's language provides the antidote to the problem the poem describes. To exercise restraint in the face of catastrophe, to refuse the glamour of its occasion, is not to insulate oneself from self-congratulation (no work of art is completely immune to that) but to pause before the arrogance of understanding, the contentedness of having met the challenge of what should not be met. The diction of Stevens's poem is like the natural world in poems like "The Death of a Soldier": whatever is happening, the diction goes, nevertheless, in its direction. There is not only, as I have suggested so far, a sternness in nature's refusal to acknowledge human suffering; there is also immense consolation—the assurance that the natural world will prevail in spite of the human potential for destruction. The language of Stevens's poetry partakes, in small ways, of this consolation.

To say so is not to take a stand against poems containing open references to war or shop windows. MacNeice was correct when he maintained that Yeats's "Lake Isle of Innisfree" would have been different, neither better nor worse, if it bore the signs of its occasion. Similarly, Stevens's poems alert us to the fact that every poem assumes a position in relationship to its occasion, even if its language may seem not to acknowledge that occasion. Sometimes even sophisticated readers mistake reference for relevance, assuming that a poem referring openly to public events is automatically responsible to those events. But such a poem may be responsible, or it may not; so may or may not a poem that eschews topical reference.

"What do you think the responsibilities of writers in general are when and if war comes," Stevens was asked in 1939. "A war is a military state of affairs," he responded, "not a literary one." Read out of context, these stringent remarks might seem to suggest that Stevens believed that poetry can muster no authentic relationship to public experience. In fact, these remarks are evidence of Stevens's relentless consideration of that relationship, a relationship that by its very nature must be troubled, tenuous, delicate, inconsistent, registered in language that is itself by nature troubled and tenuous. To assert that war is not a literary affair is like asserting that seasonal change is not a literary affair: no poem exists in a happy oblivion, but to believe we have fulfilled our social responsibilities simply by writing poems is a sentimentality Stevens could not countenance. Whitman might as readily have said that infinitude is not a literary affair, Dickinson that the self is not a literary affair. Such refusals are the mark of engagement.

The Visible Core

What constitutes a confessional poem? What allows us to imagine that a poem's language has an authentic relationship not to public but to private experience? Today, while the word *confession* might be associated with certain poems by Dickinson, Yeats, or even Eliot, the word is associated most indelibly with Robert Lowell's *Life Studies*, published in 1959. Yet Lowell himself disliked the word, using it only once in an ultimately discarded stanza of "Waking Early Sunday Morning," published in 1965.

> Time to grub up and junk the year's
> output, a dead wood of dry verse:
> dim confession, coy revelation,
> liftings, listless self-imitation,
> whole days when I could hardly speak,
> came pluming home unshaven, weak
> and willing to read anyone
> things done before and better done.

"Dim confession, coy revelation," says Lowell not of his legion of imitators but of his imitations of himself. For Lowell, a revelatory poem was not automatically intimate because he knew that confessionalism is more primarily a style of writing than a relationship to subject matter; he understood that language has no inevitable relationship to experience of any kind. But the style of *Life Studies* made it seem as if language could sustain such a relationship, and in the book's powerful wake, subsequent poets adopted Lowell's style—the flattened rhythms, the avoidance of egregiously figurative language—as an all-purpose way of denoting experience. What was artifice to Lowell became a way of inhabiting the language of American poetry at large, and, in the process, received poetic forms came to resemble what Adrienne Rich called "asbestos gloves," tools a poet must supposedly discard in order to handle experience more directly.

By the time this happened, Lowell had transformed himself again. The stanza from "Waking Early Sunday Morning" sounds like Lowell, but it does not sound exactly like the Lowell of *Life Studies*, the book in which Lowell so publicly dramatized his movement from meter and rhyme to free verse, and neither does it sound exactly like the Lowell of *Lord Weary's Castle*, the early book in which a fervid embrace of meter and rhyme first made Lowell famous.

> I saw the sky descending, black and white,
> Not blue, on Boston, where the winters wore
> The skulls to jack-o'-lanterns on the slates,
> And Hunger's skin-and-bone retrievers tore
> The chickadee and shrike.

The difference between this passage from "Where the Rainbow Ends" and the passage from "Waking Early Sunday Morning" is not the fact of meter and rhyme, which the passages share, but a quality of diction (colloquial versus hieratic) and figure (mundane versus apocalyptic) that makes "Waking Early Sunday Morning" feel less oracular than intimate, the language corresponding to our given notions of what constitutes a vulnerable relationship to experience. Where did Lowell learn to produce such language?

"Really I've just broken through to where you've always been," he wrote to Elizabeth Bishop after writing the poems of *Life Studies*, but while Bishop's example was crucial to Lowell and therefore to the recent history of American poetry, the relationship between these two poets was far more complicated—frustrated by jealousy, challenged by mental illness—than this remark suggests. Over the thirty years of their friendship, Bishop and Lowell saw each other only rarely (Bishop lived in Brazil from 1951 to 1967), and their meetings often released an emotional intensity that is difficult to parse; the meetings tended to coincide with Lowell's manic breakdowns, and on more than one occasion he confessed to Bishop that she was the true love of his life. Both poets strove, in very different but provocatively overlapping ways, to forge a language of intimacy in their poems, and the intimacy between the poets themselves—an intimacy that developed through language—was at once the subject of and the fuel for the language of their poems.

Bishop and Lowell first met at a dinner party given by their mutual friend Randall Jarrell. Their correspondence began immediately thereafter—with mildly entertaining trivialities. Bishop to Lowell, 14 August 1947:

> I was called out to see a calf being born in the pasture beside the house. In five minutes after several falls on its nose it was standing up and shaking its head & tail & trying to nurse. They took it away from its mother almost immediately & carried it struggling in a wheelbarrow to the barn—we've just been watching it trying to lie down. Once up it didn't know how to get down again & finally fell in a heap.

Behind this letter lies not only the Jarrell dinner party but also Lowell's review of Bishop's first book, *North & South*, which appeared in the *Sewanee Review* in the summer of 1947. "Her admirers are not likely to hail her as a giant among the moderns," wrote Lowell, "or to compare anything that she will ever write with Shakespeare or Donne. Nevertheless, the splendor and minuteness of her descriptions soon seem wonderful." Bishop's self-consciously charming letter plays to Lowell's praise—as if she were eager to prove that, while she'd never be Shakespeare or Donne, she's spot-on about dairy farming.

Given the prominence that Bishop has accrued since her death in 1979, it is difficult to remember that she spent her entire career standing in the shadow of Robert Traill Spence Lowell Jr., who was infinitely more famous than she—the kind of poet known by people who don't read poetry. By 1947 Lowell had already won his first Pulitzer Prize, for *Lord Weary's Castle*, and in the sixties, while Bishop was living in Brazil, publishing infrequently, Lowell was refusing invitations to the Johnson White House and appearing on the cover of *Time* magazine. By that time Bishop had also won important prizes, but she remained (in John Ashbery's admiring phrase) a "writer's writer's writer," and her wariness around Lowell, whom she also loved, took different forms over time.

In 1948 Lowell forwarded to Bishop these remarks about her poems by the Harvard philosopher George Santayana: "I *liked* 'North & South' especially for its delicacy. If it were not for the Darky Woman who is looking for a husband that shall be monogamous [in 'Songs for a Colored Singer'], I should have thought that Elizabeth Bishop had little sense of reality." Bishop responded that she was "delighted" with Santayana's insensitive remarks, but that hardly seems possible. She parried by sending Lowell these remarks by her friend Margaret Miller, a curator at the Museum of Modern Art: "I have never read a word of R. L. and had suspected that at least a portion of your enthusiasm for the poetry could be laid to professional politeness. I was therefore unprepared for all that blacktongued piratical vigor. I can't read more than three or four poems at a sitting—it's a little like smelling salts—but they are remarkable and wonderful, though the rhymes seem a little *too* strong or crass on occasions."

This is a keenly perceptive account of the poems of *Lord Weary's Castle*, which are as aggressively apocalyptic as the poems of *North & South* are retiringly descriptive. But description was for Bishop a very complicated and often calculated enterprise, as both her poems and her letters reveal: "The water looks like blue gas—the harbor is always a mess, here, junky little boats all piled up, some hung with sponges and always a few half sunk or splintered up from the most recent hurricane. It reminds me a little of my desk." Bishop sent this account of the harbor at Key West to Lowell in 1948, and a year later she reported that she'd "sold the *New Yorker* a medium length bit of plain description." She was referring to her poem "The Bight," which grew from her letter about Key West and is anything but a bit of plain description—though the poem's characteristically low-keyed dilation of the act of description makes it seem so.

> There is a fence of chicken wire along the dock
> where, glinting like little plowshares,
> the blue-gray shark tails are hung up to dry
> for the Chinese-restaurant trade.
> Some of the little white boats are still piled up
> against each other, or lie on their sides, stove in,
> and not yet salvaged, if they ever will be, from the last
>   bad storm,
> like torn-open, unanswered letters.

The bight is littered with old correspondences.
Click. Click. Goes the dredge,
and brings up a dripping jawful of marl.
All the untidy activity continues,
awful but cheerful.

These lines are about the power of description, about how meticulous attention to the surface of things inevitably dredges up emotional depths. The point of "The Bight" is not merely to offer an account of a dilapidated harbor but also to dramatize a state of mind that finds itself mirrored in such dilapidation. The poem is subtitled "On my birthday," and its final line ("awful but cheerful") appears by Bishop's request on her tombstone. Her characterization of "The Bight" as a "bit of plain description" only reinforces the poem's strategy of reticent understatement, and her motive in employing that characterization to Lowell is difficult to read. Was her coyness an invitation to her private world, a world she needed simultaneously to construct and to conceal? Or did she think that the purveyor of blacktongued piratical vigor would be deaf to such subtle gestures of intimacy?

I suspect the latter. Lowell to Bishop, 16 August 1948: "If you'd come to Ipswich—you'd have found waiting for you: Anne Dick, Elliott and Mrs. Chandler, the woman who almost converted Mrs. Sortwell, and my first project for you: age 41, weight: 155, hair: full black graying. He has lived for 20 years in a spic and span little white house with two aged servants tending lambs and reading Thoreau and writing a book which no one has seen." Lowell's "project" was to find Bishop (who was not yet acknowledging her lesbianism publicly) a husband. Bishop to Lowell: "I think you've done an enormous amount of groundwork already & I can see I picked the right person to solve my problems about my future for me." Was she serious? Bishop to Carley Dawson, Lowell's ex-girlfriend, a few days later: "If I want to remain friends with Cal at all, I'd better not see him for some time."

Behind this exchange lurks a mysterious but emotionally momentous day that Bishop and Lowell spent together in Stonington, Maine, in the summer of 1948. Lowell had arrived in Stonington with Dawson, Bishop with Tom Wanning, whose relationship to Bishop remains unclear. But after a few days, Dawson left with Wanning, leaving Lowell and Bishop alone. They talked, they went swimming: Lowell decided he wanted to marry Bishop himself. Nine years later, in 1957, after a manic breakdown reawakened this fantasy, Lowell explained his embarrassing behavior by reaching back to "that long swimming and sunning Stonington day after Carley's removal by Tommy":

> I was feeling the infected hollowness of the Carley business draining out of my heart, and you said rather humorously yet it was truly meant, "When you write my epitaph, you must say I was the loneliest person who ever lived." Probably you forget, and anyway all that is mercifully changed and all has come right since you found Lota. But at the time . . . our relations seemed to have reached a new place. I assumed that would be just a matter of time before I proposed and I half believed that you would accept. . . . But asking you is *the* might have been for me, the one towering change, the other life that might have been had.

This kind of frankness was unusual even after Lowell and Bishop had known each other for many years. They communicated most intimately by indirection, by emblem, by letters that feel

self-consciously like literature rather than an unfettered exchange between friends. Bishop did not respond to Lowell's confession, though she fussed over a pointlessly detailed account of
a sailing expedition that Lowell used as a way of ramping up to
the confession.

The phrase *confessional poetry* was first coined by the poet
M. L. Rosenthal in a review of Lowell's *Life Studies*. Bishop
came to dislike the phrase as much as Lowell did, but when she
first read the poems of *Life Studies* she did immediately register what she called their "strangely modest tone"—"they are all
about yourself and yet do not sound conceited!" What Bishop
could not have known was that, in the wake of his 1957 breakdown, Lowell discovered this tone by writing poems about
Bishop, spoken by Bishop, or emulating Bishop's sensibility. He
was obsessed. "Skunk Hour," modeled on Bishop's "Armadillo,"
came first, and it was followed swiftly by poems that adapt
Bishop's way of rendering emotional states by seeming merely
to account for the surface of things.

> In my Father's bedroom:
> blue threads as thin
> as pen-writing on the bedspread,
> blue dots on the curtains,
> a blue kimono,
> Chinese sandals with blue plush straps.
> The broad-planked floor
> had a sandpapered neatness.
> The clear glass bed-lamp
> with a white doily shade
> was still raised a few
> inches by resting on volume two
> of Lafcadio Hearn's

> *Glimpses of unfamiliar Japan.*
> Its warped olive cover
> was punished like a rhinoceros hide.

That book will never be opened, no unfamiliar glimpses will be had. Similarly, the diction of Lowell's strategically flat poem will account only for surfaces, but we feel the sharp poignancy of unrecognized depth, of life unlived.

While Lowell told Bishop, apropos of the poems of *Life Studies,* that he had broken through to where she'd always been, he also traveled to places where she'd never go. *The Dolphin,* Lowell's 1973 book about the end of his marriage to Elizabeth Hardwick, provoked famously troubled objections from Bishop—objections that were rehearsed more quietly but with great precision when she found herself in Lowell's poems. In this draft, written in 1957 when Lowell was in the midst of *Life Studies,* the speaker is meant to be Bishop herself.

> Starlike the eagle on my locket watch,
> Mother's sole heirloom. I hear her, "All I want
> To do is kill you!"—I, a child of four;
> She, early American and militant.

Bishop's mother was committed permanently to a sanatorium in 1916, when Bishop was five. Bishop to Lowell, with studied nonchalance: "While I remember it—one small item I may have mentioned before. If you ever do anything with that poem about me, would you change the remark my mother was supposed to have made? She never did make it; in fact, I don't remember any direct threats, except the usual maternal ones. Her danger for me was just implied in the things I overheard the grown-ups say before and after her disappearance."

Bishop had written about her mother's mental illness in her

story "In the Village," but her method (as in her letters and poems) was implication, not hyperbole; it's hard to imagine Bishop putting the aggrandizing modifier *sole* in front of *heirloom*, much less literalizing the implied danger of her mother's behavior in a direct threat. Remaking his style in the poems of *Life Studies*, Lowell learned from Bishop how to let description create the aura of intimacy, but the apocalyptic Lowell of *Lord Weary's Castle* was never completely tamed, and, unlike Bishop, Lowell ultimately gravitated toward ominous rather than ordinary details: to call his poems nothing but "plain description" would seem inappropriate, not coy, since the poems always seem clearly to be more than that. This is why the style of *Life Studies* could become massively influential, an immediately identifiable turning point in literary history, while the power of Bishop's style could remain for a long time underestimated, unlikely to produce poems worthy of Shakespeare and Donne.

Since Lowell's death and the simultaneous decline in the prestige of confessional poetry, however, the apparently reticent Bishop has been used as a club to beat the apparently revelatory Lowell, much as Lowell was once used as a club to beat the apparently impersonal T. S. Eliot. Yet to varying degrees, both Lowell's and Bishop's poems embody a tension between reticence and revelation, a tension crucial to any art that might otherwise seem merely reticent or merely revelatory. At their most alluring, Bishop's poems lean dangerously toward the former quality while Lowell's lean toward the latter, and for both poets, what is truly at stake is not the act of revelation as such but the style in which that act is dramatized.

No one would mistake a letter by Robert Lowell for a letter by Elizabeth Bishop, just as no one could confuse their poems. But while Bishop's letters to Lowell can seem strategic in their dependence on charm, her poems never do, though they threaten to seem as if they might. And while Lowell's letters can seem bullying, his poems threaten to seem so especially when they surprise us with tenderness. The success of their styles depends, as style does, on the transformation of a poet's characteristic limitation into a power that stops short of becoming a method, a power that remains conversant with the possibility of its own failure. "In the end / the water was too cold for us," wrote Lowell in "Water," a poem about the strange intimacy he and Bishop shared one day in Maine, a day that neither poet had a language to speak of.

The Opposite of Risk

"Frank O'Hara's poetry has no program and therefore cannot be joined," said John Ashbery after the death of his friend in 1966. Both O'Hara and Ashbery were associated with what became known as the New York School of poets; in the decades that followed, Ashbery would find his own poems determining contemporary taste with a power that, in recent literary history, only the poems of Lowell and Eliot had assumed. But Ashbery took pains to assert the radical individuality not only of O'Hara's poetry but also, by implication, of his own. The "avoidance of anything like a program . . . is not just a characteristic of the New York School," he insisted, "but of poetry in general, if by poetry you mean Keats or Spenser or Chaucer or Whitman or Rimbaud." Refusing to see poetry merely in the light of recent literary history, Ashbery cast his net widely, confounding any sense of art as a program that might be spurned or joined.

Neither would he justify O'Hara's poetry in the light of recent political history: "It does not advocate sex and dope as a panacea for the ills of modern society; it does not speak out against the war in Vietnam or in favor of civil rights; it does not paint gothic vignettes of the post-Atomic age." Writing these sentences in 1966 was like waving a red cape, and the bull appeared in the form of the poet Louis Simpson, who accused Ashbery of "sneering at the conscience of other poets." But Ashbery was not sneering; he was discriminating between true social commitment and the programmatic manners of commitment, manners with which a poem might too easily congratulate itself. He confronted Simpson as stalwartly as the Stevens who on the eve of World War II asserted that war is a military affair, not a literary affair: "Poetry is poetry. Protest is protest. I believe in both forms of action."

No one committed to the act of writing poems—weighing syllables, calibrating lines, negotiating syntax—could avoid feeling a little shy about the need to assert that poetry is poetry, and Ashbery's most characteristic tone is shyness, not confrontation. Shortly before O'Hara's death, he had returned to the United States after a decade spent living in France, and in contrast to the world of American poetry he remembered from his youth, contemporary American poetry now seemed to him oppressively dour. And if it wasn't dour, it was hysterical. And if it managed to be playful, it seemed sanctimonious, tilting against the windmills of the establishment. A lost world of American poetry, an undivided world in which "poets spoke different dialects of a common poetic language," seemed to him far more attractive. What he missed in the America to which he returned was a particular sound, "a peculiar, resonant blend of metaphysical poetry and Surrealism which was typical of much of the advanced poetry written in America in the late thirties and forties—a fine and touching moment in our poetry that has so far been little noticed by subsequent critics."

Who produced that sound? Why was Ashbery attracted to it?

> Some of the sky is grey and some of it is white.
> The leaves have lost their heads
> And are dancing around the tree in circles, dead;
> The cat is in it.

A smeared, banged, tow-headed
Girl in a flowered, flour-sack print
Sniffles and holds up her last bite
Of bread and butter and brown sugar to the wind.

Butter the cat's paws
And bread the wind. We are moving.

This is early Randall Jarrell, the unrelievedly tender poet who opened the young Ashbery's ears to the music of shyness. The poem's plain sense is liberated into what Elizabeth Bishop called the surrealism of everyday life—the leaves have lost their heads, the cat's paws are buttered—and even a simple line like "The cat is in it" feels spooky, its pronoun untethered from the tree to which it refers. But while the poem is in motion, its tone is steady: these lines are not spoken by the little girl, but we feel that her sensibility guides their waywardness, allowing us to glimpse the secret, tentative confusions of a child's inner world.

This is late Ashbery, the Ashbery of the twenty-first century.

One afternoon as golden stalks
grazed the parlor of heaven
the little shift in tone came
to tell us to get ready
to pack enough things
                    The blue sky screeched
                    A father and his daughter were
                        passing
                    the corner of the delighted crescent
Don't blame me for the stuff of change
        I too carry
        I think I'll go in now

Unlike Jarrell, Ashbery does not psychologize his wayward-ness, associating the movement of the language with the movement of a child's mind. But his quiet, unquestioning acceptance of the world as it comes to him is like a child's: the poem feels deferential, restrained, embarrassed by its own capacity for wonder. The tone is variable enough to include moments of disgruntlement ("Don't blame me"), but the poem's pieces are stitched together by a sensibility that does not confuse submission with resignation, shyness with powerlessness. When the golden stalks graze the parlor of heaven, he packs his bags. He enjoys the little things glimpsed along the way, the blue sky, the delighted crescent. And if he feels a little confused, a little out of sorts, he'd rather not admit it; he knows we feel that way too, and he trusts us to recognize his feelings. A "little shift in tone" can tell us everything. After all, he's talking about mortality, the same thing he's been talking about for fifty years, except that it feels imminent now, around the next bend.

The passage of time has always been Ashbery's subject: his poems embody the sweet bewilderment they also describe. But in retrospect, the poems from his first great period are more guarded. Throughout the volumes of the midsixties to seventies (*The Double Dream of Spring, Self-Portrait in a Convex Mirror, Houseboat Days*), a whiff of preachiness accompanies the moments as they pass.

> This was our ambition: to be small and clear and free.
> Alas, the summer's energy wanes quickly,
> A moment and it is gone. And no longer
> May we make the necessary arrangements, simple as
>   they are.

This need to allegorize the poetry's waywardness was long gone by the time Ashbery wrote his poems of the late twentieth century. In its place we find a giddiness that makes the earlier work sound, by comparison, almost stodgy.

> There's a story here about a kind of grass that grows in
>   the Amazon
> valley that is too tall for birds to fly over—
> they fly past it instead—
> yet leeches have no trouble navigating its circuitous
>   heaps
> and are wont to throw celebratory banquets afterward,
> at which awards are given out—best costume in a period
>   piece
> too distracted by the rapids to notice what period it is,
>   and so on.
> Before retiring the general liked to play a game of all-
>   white dominoes,
> after which he would place his nightcap distractedly on
>   the other man's crocheted chamber-pot lid.
> Subsiding into a fitful slumber, warily he dreams
> of the giant hand descended from heaven
> like the slope of a moraine, whose fingers were bedizened
>   with rings
> in which every event that had ever happened in the uni-
>   verse could sometimes be discerned.

The point of these two passages is pretty much the same, but in these lines from *Chinese Whispers* Ashbery merely celebrates the passage of time, leaving the preachiness behind. His sentences have become longer, his syntax more elegantly attenuated, his diction more egregiously varied. But while the poems are showier, they seem less like the work of a show-off. They sound happy to exist, rather than needing to be justified.

Rogue moments of tenderness often break through the giddiness of these poems, no sooner glimpsed than gone. In contrast, Ashbery's achievement in the most recent work is to have found a way to let the tenderness dominate entire poems, even an entire volume of poems, without sacrificing the wayward, effortlessly disjunctive texture that has always distinguished him. The title of *Where Shall I Wander*, the book that inaugurated this late phase of his career, is lifted from Mother Goose ("Goosey goosey gander, / Whither shall I wander?"), and every poem is infused with the combination of tenderness and menace that we associate with nursery rhymes. In "Coma Berenices," a parody of a family's annual Christmas letter, Ashbery's ear for the comic potential of inarticulate writing is acute, but this master of tone is not sneering. The exquisitely turned awkwardness of these sentences is a vehicle for emotional transparency.

> Summer was quiet except for the usual "transients." Fran and Don stopped by on their way to the traditional games in the Scottish highlands. They are centuries old and an amazing sight, it seems. Each sent a card from Scotland. Mary and her little boy came by in August. We went to the fish place but I'm not sure if Lance (her boy) appreciated it. Children have such pronounced tastes and can be quite stubborn about it. In late September a high point was the autumn foliage which was magnificent this year. Casper took me and his wife's two aunts on a "leaf-peeping" trip in northern Vermont. We were near Canada but

didn't actually cross the border. You can get the same souvenir junk on this side for less money Max said. He is such a card.

November. Grief over Nancy Smith.

Where Shall I Wander is a book not of grief displayed or avoided but of grief inhabited in a plainly matter-of-fact way, as if it were a familiar side dish at every meal. "We went down gently / to the bottom-most step," says the book's opening poem. "There you can grieve and breathe, / rinse your possessions in the chilly spring." There's no illusion that our youth was free of grief, and neither is there any longing to be rid of it. Nostalgia has always been a temptation for Ashbery, and I suspect that at times the giddiness has been a way to stave off the potential sentimentality of longing. In an earlier poem, the question "We're still here, aren't we?" might feel ironic, but in *Where Shall I Wander* it feels sweet, as if it were written in the whispery language the mind speaks to itself as it's falling asleep. Now, Ashbery is a poet of the present, and he requires fewer defenses.

"He was writing in an age in which the most natural feeling of tenderness, happiness, or sorrow was likely to be called sentimental; consequently he needed a self-protective rhetoric as the most brutal or violent of poets did not." Randall Jarrell made this remark apropos of his teacher, John Crowe Ransom, but he might as well have been talking about himself or, if he'd lived long enough, about Ashbery.

What constitutes such a rhetoric?

> But though I have wept and fasted, wept and prayed,
> Though I have seen my head brought in upon a platter,
> I am no prophet.
> I have seen the moment of my greatness flicker,

> And I have seen the eternal Footman hold my coat,
> And in short, I was afraid.

These lines from T. S. Eliot's "The Love Song of J. Alfred Prufrock" are threatened with an overflow of feeling. But something is missing here: transcribing the lines, I've left out the asides ("grown slightly bald," "and here's no great matter," "and snicker") with which the early Eliot salts his syntax.

> But though I have wept and fasted, wept and prayed
> Though I have seen my head [grown slightly bald] brought
>   in upon a platter,
> I am no prophet—and here's no great matter;
> I have seen the moment of my greatness flicker,
> And I have seen the eternal Footman hold my coat, and
>   snicker,
> And in short, I was afraid.

Here, the simple statement "I was afraid" sounds completely different from how it sounds in the version of "Prufrock" I've constructed without the ironic asides; it sounds poignant, like Ashbery's question in *Where Shall I Wander*—"We're still here, aren't we?"

I don't mean to suggest that "Prufrock" is a better poem without the asides, far from it: Eliot deployed a self-protective rhetoric not to distance himself from overpowering emotion but to allow those emotions into the poem. Up until the end of the twentieth century, Ashbery often employed shifts in diction for the same purpose, especially when he was writing about sexuality.

> When it was over no one had the courage to come out
>   into the daylight,
> or knew there was any. I fell asleep

on a sandhill, and dreamed this, and gave it to you, and
    you thanked me, solemnly,
but we were not permitted to associate, only to corre-
    spond, and you came out
to me again, as we wished one another good afternoon,
    and then went away
again into the fog-lit embrasure.

These lines from *Girls on the Run*, with their suggestion of for-
bidden sexual intimacy, make audible the lyrical sweetness that
underlies Ashbery's music at all times. But immediately following these lines Ashbery interrupts himself ("Where was I?")
and begins nattering about "jelly-bean screw-drivers" and "shopping tours to East Testicle." Here, like the early Eliot, he allows
the sweetness to linger by threatening to let it sour.

Would the poem of pure sweetness, the poem liberated from
a protective rhetoric, be driven by shyness or boldness? Writing
about shyness in children, the psychoanalyst D. W. Winnicott
points out that shyness is by no means an inevitable liability,
though it can become one. What is more troublesome is the child
who is insufficiently shy, the child who is consequently praised by
adults for seeming preternaturally grown-up. Such a child suffers, says Winnicott, from a lack of imagination: "There are fear-
ful things inside such a child, as there are inside others, but he
cannot risk finding them outside, cannot let his imagination run
away with him." Just as the representation of chaos in art is inevitably the result of a self-conscious ordering of the medium, just
as excess is a product of restraint, so is the rhetoric of shyness
dependent upon decisive aesthetic decisions—on great imaginative capacity.

These sentences conclude the title poem of *Where Shall I
Wander*.

Invading the privacy of millions with a lurid bed-
time story, the little dog laughs, climbs the stepstool
bearing red carnations and lapses. The laughter begins slowly at the bottom of the orchestra pit and
wells gradually toward the back; it seems to say
it's OK not to be counted, you'll belong eventually
even if you're not wearing the right armband or
redingote. I crawled through a culvert to get here
and you're right to love me, I was only a little awry,
now it's my fancy to be here and with you, alright,
fluted, not toxic. Prepare the traditional surprise
banquet of braised goat.

You wore your cummerbund with the stars and
stripes. I, kilted in lime, held a stethoscope to the
head of the parting guest. Together we were a
couple forever.

This passage is distinguished by Ashbery's infallible ear for the
wildly various levels of diction that the English language affords
him, a string of words derived from French (*prepare, traditional,
surprise, banquet, braised*) upended by the bluntly Anglo-Saxon
goat. He even pulls a French word (*redingote*) derived from a
pair of English words (*riding coat*) back into the English language. But while harnessing the natural disjunctiveness of our
language, twisting and turning from bedroom to concert hall to
culvert, Ashbery does not deploy these shifts in diction to de-
flect us from the emotion toward which the passage builds. The
ironies don't undermine the improbable feeling of having been
loved despite one's peculiarities and flaws. Instead, the language
feels as improbable as a love that survives the peculiarities and
flaws of the world at large, a world in which everything is always
a little awry, a world in which no one is ever wearing just the

right clothes, a world in which long-lasting love feels like grace. The emotional transparency of the final sentence of *Where Shall I Wander*—"Together we were a couple forever"—feels simultaneously surprising and inevitable, foreseeable yet always about to be known.

"This is a long way from the ironic style, since the doubling exists within the evidence," says Ellen Bryant Voigt of a poem by Emily Dickinson, "not in performative response or preemptive protection." Though she does not come right out and say so, Voigt deploys the phrase "ironic style" to describe the world after Ashbery, a world in which a legion of imitators have by and large gone after the preachiness or giddiness that were more prominent in Ashbery's earlier work, transforming it into a method and ignoring the essential shyness that has fueled both Ashbery's deployment and his dismissal of these protective rhetorics. In the way that Lowell once did, Ashbery has dominated the American poetic landscape for the past several decades, but just as very few poets harnessed what was truly most powerful in Lowell, very few poets actually sound like Ashbery, sound at once confident and vulnerable, sophisticated and awkward, bold and shy. For more of that sound, we need to listen to both the living and the dead.

Poetry Thinking

Near the end of *The Tempest*, when everything finally seems to be going well, the exiled magician Prospero stages a pageant, a play within the play, to celebrate the impending marriage of his daughter, Miranda, to Ferdinand, the prince of Naples. "Let me live here ever," says young Ferdinand, entranced by the performance. But suddenly the play stops—Prospero has had a thought, one that cannot be ignored: Caliban is still plotting Prospero's death.

"Our revels now are ended," says Prospero to the startled Ferdinand.

> These our actors,
> As I foretold you, were all spirits and
> Are melted into air, into thin air;
> And, like the baseless fabric of this vision,
> The cloud-capped tow'rs, the gorgeous palaces,
> The solemn temples, the great globe itself,
> Yea, all which it inherit, shall dissolve,
> And, like this insubstantial pageant faded,
> Leave not a rack behind. We are such stuff
> As dreams are made on, and our little life
> Is rounded with a sleep.

What has happened to Prospero's sudden alarm? Rather than running off to subvert Caliban's plot, he ruminates on the illusion he has created, the play itself, and his thoughts move from the impermanence of artistic creation to the impermanence of human life. Then another thought pierces him.

> Sir, I am vexed.
> Bear with my weakness: my old brain is troubled.
> Be not disturbed with my infirmity.
> If you be pleased, retire into my cell,
> And there repose. A turn or two I'll walk
> To still my beating mind.

Does Prospero need to take a stroll because he's upset about Caliban? No, that once urgent thought has passed, like the pageant it interrupted. Instead, Prospero has been shaken by his unexpected thoughts about mortality. Who could have heard it coming?

Thinking in poetry it what turns us, changes us, makes us move. This is why all the great speeches in Shakespeare feel like dramatizations of the mind in motion; the speakers are as surprised by their own thoughts as we are. And this, in turn, is why we feel so acutely that we know Shakespeare's characters from the inside out, as if we were listening to their minds. In Shakespeare, all brains worth listening to are troubled. Prospero's thinking is undone by thinking itself, the unpredictably shifting process through which the beating mind becomes audible to itself over time.

This sound echoes everywhere in our poetry, from Shakespeare to Ashbery and beyond, but it is not often heard in the verse of Shakespeare's contemporaries. When did Shakespeare learn to produce it? *The Tempest* was the last play he wrote without a collaborator, and in his very earliest plays no one speaks his mind as Prospero does. Speaking here in *The Third Part of Henry the Sixth* is Richard, Duke of Gloucester, who will become Richard III and dominate the play subsequently named for him.

> Why, I can smile, and murder whiles I smile,
> And cry "Content!" to that which grieves my heart,
> And wet my cheeks with artificial tears,
> And frame my face to all occasions.
> I'll drown more sailors than the mermaid shall;
> I'll slay more gazers than the basilisk;
> I'll play the orator as well as Nestor,
> Deceive more slily than Ulysses could,
> And, like a Sinon, take another Troy.
> I can add colors to the chameleon,
> Change shapes with Proteus for advantages,
> And set the murderous Machiavel to school.
> Can I do this, and cannot get a crown?
> Tut, were it farther off, I'll pluck it down.

Richard is touting his prowess as an actor, a role-player, a shape-changer. His language registers the newfound power of selfhood that we associate with the Renaissance, when the very word *self* ceased to be merely a reflexive and took on the now familiar sense (as the *O.E.D.* puts it) of a person who is "really and intrinsically *he*." Such a self immediately becomes capable of thinking of itself as other than itself, protean, a murderer who smiles, a happy man who weeps.

But there is nothing protean about the way Richard speaks. The passage I've quoted from his speech is made of five sentences: the first three are from three to five lines long, and each begins with a clause that establishes the grammatical template for the parallel syntax to follow (*I can smile—I'll drown more sailors—I can add colors*). Then the speech concludes with two one-line sentences that have the gathering force of a sonnet's final couplet:

"Can I do this, and cannot get a crown? / Tut, were it farther off, I'll pluck it down." Unlike Prospero's final words, which surprise him as much as they do us, this conclusion feels willed. Richard comprehends the power of metamorphosis, but his speech does not embody that power. This mind is standing still.

Part of the thrill of Richard's malevolence is due to the creepily static quality of his character. But none of Shakespeare's greatest characters speak the language of completed thought, not even his most conniving villains. Their language embodies the process through which thoughts are not organized but discovered, a process that feels at once at odds with itself and generated by itself, a process for which Coleridge offered this brilliant metaphor, in order to distinguish Shakespeare from his more declamatory contemporaries: "Shakespeare goes on creating, and evolving B. out of A., and C. out of B., and so on, just as a serpent moves, which makes a fulcrum of its own body, and seems for ever twisting and untwisting its own strength." This drama of discovery, as unpredictably linear as it is purposeful, is what we feel in the speech of all the great characters of Shakespeare's maturity—and in many of the minor characters too. It is also what we feel in the great lyric poems of our language.

"What has thou been?" asks King Lear of Edgar, the unjustly reviled son of Gloucester, who plays the role of Tom o' Bedlam when he joins the outcast Lear on the heath. Like Richard, Edgar assumes the power of pretense, but he speaks with a rigorous charisma that Richard doesn't attain. I've spoken of the virtues of dilation in Shakespeare, and here, Edgar's inflated response to Lear's simple question feels larger than the scene provoking it, as if the individual will were as vast as language itself.

> A servingman, proud in heart and mind; that
> curled my hair, wore gloves in my cap; served the

lust of my mistress' heart, and did the act of dark-
ness with her; swore as many oaths as I spake
words, and broke them in the sweet face of heaven.
One that slept in the contriving of lust, and waked
to do it. Wine loved I deeply, dice dearly, and in
woman out-paramoured the Turk. False of heart,
light of ear, bloody of hand; hog in sloth, fox in
stealth, wolf in greediness, dog in madness, lion in
prey. Let not the creaking of shoes nor the rustling
of silks betray thy poor heart to woman. Keep thy
foot out of brothels, thy hand out of plackets, thy
pen from lenders' books, and defy the foul fiend.
Still through the hawthorn blows the cold wind;
says suum, mun, nonny.

Although it is cast in what might seem to be the looser decorum of prose, Edgar's speech is structured sturdily—as sturdily
as Richard's is except that its repetitions do not consolidate but
complicate the meaning as the speech unfolds, asking us to review and rethink. First the speech offers a list of all the bravura
roles this role-player has played (servingman, hair-curler, glove-
wearer, adulterer, defamer, wine-lover), a list that crests in a de-
liciously excessive second list of the animal qualities displayed
in each of these performances: "hog in sloth, fox in stealth, wolf
in greediness, dog in madness, lion in prey." Then the speech offers another list of parallel clauses, but the mood shifts from the
declarative to the imperative ("Keep thy foot out of brothels,
thy hand out of plackets"), as if suddenly to suggest that this
wastrel's life is to be not glorified but condemned. Finally, out
of these considered warnings erupts an unprecedented lyricism
("Still through the hawthorn blows the cold wind") that quickly
segues into pure sound ("suum, mun, nonny"). The whole speech

moves with the interlaced energy of surprise and inevitability that distinguishes alert conversation, and, as a result, the speech feels driven by forces larger than a single speaker's intention to express what he already knows. The language functions as the fulcrum of itself. It seems to be performing Edgar as much as Edgar is performing Tom. It embodies the kind of thinking that in *King Lear* gets things done.

Thinking, as Heidegger describes it in his *Discourse on Thinking*, may take one of two forms: calculative thinking, which is driven by the will, and meditative thinking, which enables and is enabled by an openness to the mystery of existence. Richard is a calculative thinker, Edgar a meditative thinker— but only when he assumes the guise of Tom o' Bedlam. For when Edgar drops the guise he reverts to given wisdom: "When we our betters see bearing our woes, / We scarcely think our miseries our foes," he says after his encounter with Lear on the heath. This kind of willed language, based on the presupposition of justice and proportion in the universe, is precisely what *King Lear* beats to nothingness.

It is also the kind of language we first hear from the mouth of Lear himself, who begins the play as a calculative thinker— which is to say that, in a sense, he is not thinking at all. After he's exiled to the heath, Lear must go deeper than Edgar: he must learn truly to think, to surprise himself—which is a way of saying that, in the narrowly prescribed psychic economy of the play, Lear goes mad.

> They flattered me like a dog, and told me I had the white hairs in my beard ere the black ones were there. To say "ay" and "no" to everything that I said! "Ay" and "no" too was no good divinity. When the rain came to wet me once, and the wind to make

me chatter; when the thunder would not peace at
my bidding, there I found 'em, there I smelt 'em
out. Go to, they are not men o' their words. They
told me I was everything. 'Tis a lie—I am not
ague-proof.

Lear's realization here is the same as Prospero's, and it is the
simplest but most profound realization of all: he is mortal, he
too can catch cold. But Lear had to learn to sound like Tom o'
Bedlam, to become a meditative thinker, in order to achieve this
realization. At the beginning of the play, Lear's language evinces
very little interiority; he is simply walking through the role of the
benignly despotic monarch. But by the middle of the third act,
we feel, listening to Lear, that we are experiencing not only the
outward drama of self-consciously performed language but also
the inward drama of a mind remaking itself by speaking itself.

This is why the conclusion of Lear's speech on the heath ("I
am not ague-proof") does not feel merely ironic or paltry or
funny; it feels truly like something the actor playing Lear does
not know until he says it. The fourth sentence of his speech begins with a sequence of clauses delineating exterior actions (*when
the rain came, when the wind blew, when the thunder clapped*), but
the real action of the sentence is interior. And while the logic of
such thinking may initially feel occluded, it never feels puzzling.
For however disjunctive the movement of the sentences, conclusions arrive with an assurance that casts a retrospective sense of
rigor over the process by which we've reached them. This is why
the language gives us pleasure (we feel that something happens to
us at the same time that we observe something happening to the
character), and our pleasure depends not on mastery but on
submission: we feel something happen because we've trusted an
utterance we cannot yet fully comprehend.

Which is to say that we come to trust ourselves. Thinking, as Freud conceives of it, begins as preconscious activity, an activity that we paradoxically become aware of only in consciousness: whatever we know of thinking is already a representation of thinking. Listening to Shakespeare, we've learned to become conscious of what is more properly unavailable to consciousness; we've learned to imagine that his fluid enactments of interiority constitute interiority itself. And neither have we done this in isolation, for we have had other teachers who by listening to Shakespeare were themselves well taught. Milton, Wordsworth, Coleridge, Yeats, Stevens, Ashbery—between us and Shakespeare stands a long line of other poets who have trained our ears to listen for the sound of thinking. Reading poems from "Tintern Abbey" through "Sunday Morning" and beyond, we've come to expect a Shakespearean movement of mind, since, like the makers of these poems themselves, we've been taught by previous poems to imagine that our interiority is constituted in just that way.

"My Brother Tom is getting stronger," wrote Keats with heartbreaking matter-of-factness in 1818, "but his Spitting of blood continues—I sat down to read King Lear yesterday." Almost immediately Keats wrote the sonnet "On Sitting Down to Read *King Lear* Once Again," but the more consequential impact of *King Lear* was registered in letters written over the subsequent year. Having absorbed the sound of Shakespeare thinking, he set out self-consciously in his letters to mimic and, through mimicry, inhabit that sound.

> Buy a girdle—put a pebble in your Mouth—loosen your Braces—for I am going among Scenery whence I intend to tip you the Damosel Radcliffe—I'll cavern you, and grotto you, and waterfall you, and

wood you, and water you, and immense-rock you,
and tremendous sound you, and solitude you. I'll
make a lodgment on your glacis by a row of Pines,
and storm your covered way with bramble Bushes.

Keats described this kind of writing as wandering, running wild, or playing one's vagaries; yet however quixotic the energy, Keats's sentences are always as carefully constructed as Shakespeare's, the parallel syntax fueling the alliteratively driven elaboration ("waterfall you, and wood you, and water you"). Keats can sound in his letters both like Shakespeare and like a writer of prose poems from the early years of the twenty-first century. His greatest poems harness this apparently wayward energy without, given the elegance of their surface, advertising the fact that they do so.

Reading the "Ode to a Nightingale," for instance, we don't feel that the stanzas follow one another in an orderly progression toward a foreseeable conclusion; instead, we feel the poem grappling with a variety of different attitudes toward mortality, oblivion, and transcendence. Sometimes the attitudes seem merely opposed to each other, but more often they seem partially overlapping, difficult completely to distinguish from one another. The nightingale is fraught with significance, made and unmade by the luxurious music of the poem itself.

For at first, the nightingale's song seems to promise a reprieve from the human world of mortality, a world

Where palsy shakes a few, sad, last gray hairs,
Where youth grows pale, and spectre-thin, and dies;
Where but to think is to be full of sorrow.

But almost immediately the antidote to suffering perpetuates the disease. "I cannot see what flowers are at my feet," says Keats, impassioned by the nightingale's song, and the imagined flowers turn out to be as time-bound as the youth who grows pale and thin: "Fast fading violets cover'd up in leaves."

Yet the music of these lines says something else again. The gorgeous patterning of Keats's syntax, made more emphatic here by lineation (*where palsy shakes, where youth grows pale, where but to think*), invites us to take pleasure in this certain knowledge of our demise. And in no time, the very thing that the "Ode to a Nightingale" set out to evade becomes the poem's deepest wish: "Now more than ever seems it rich to die." But this wish fades as quickly as the violets that provoked it, since Keats quickly realizes that his death would not merge him with the ecstasy of the nightingale's song but sever him from it forever. The nightingale cannot perform simultaneously as a source of human pleasure and as an emblem of the obliteration of human pain. It continually eludes the function that the poem attempts to prescribe for it, and while the poem tries continually to catch up, its ultimate failure to do so feels the opposite of disheartening. The procedures of its thinking are more compelling than the conclusions, and were this not the case, the poem's final lines—

> Was it a vision, or a waking dream?
> Fled is that music:—Do I wake or sleep?

—would seem unbearably conclusive, even shallow, like the couplet rounding out Richard's speech in *Henry the Sixth*. But any answer provoked by these questions is incapable of accounting for the tissue of equivocation that constitutes our experience of the poem. Offering to summarize our experience, the questions are everywhere surpassed by it. As a result, the poem seems freshly disorienting every time we read it again. Its thinking feels as elusive, therefore as alluring, as the song of the nightingale itself.

Neither, in the world after Shakespeare, is this feeling restricted to poems.

> Mrs. Dalloway said she would buy the flowers herself.
> For Lucy had her work cut out for her. The doors would be taken off their hinges; Rumpelmayer's men were coming.

The first three sentences of *Mrs. Dalloway* twist and turn against themselves as seductively as Edgar's, but since we're used to reading stories, we experience the opening of Virginia Woolf's novel with every expectation that our questions will be answered. As a result, we might not stop to register the extraordinary leaps in thinking that these sentences demand. Who is Mrs. Dalloway? Why is she buying flowers? Why can't Lucy buy the flowers? What is Lucy doing instead? Who is Rumpelmayer? Why are they taking the doors off their hinges? I'm feeling a little uneasy. I'm scared of Rumpelmayer's men.

Reading *Mrs. Dalloway*, we quickly deduce that Clarissa, wife of Richard Dalloway, is preparing to give a party. Flowers must be bought; access between the public rooms of her home must be made simpler. The tone here is one of practiced, confident pleasure, and yet the sense of ominous discomfort unearthed by a slow reading of the novel's first three sentences is appropriate. The subsequent five sentences follow Clarissa's thoughts as she moves from the morning air around her to the air she experienced as a young woman at her family's house at Bourton to the undeniable fact that something awful was about to happen.

> Mrs. Dalloway said she would buy the flowers herself.
> For Lucy had her work cut out for her. The doors

would be taken off their hinges; Rumpelmayer's men were coming. And then, thought Clarissa Dalloway, what a morning—fresh as if issued to children on a beach.

What a lark! What a plunge! For so it had always seemed to her, when, with a little squeak on the hinges, which she could hear now, she had burst open the French windows and plunged at Bourton into the open air. How fresh, how calm, stiller than this of course, the air was in the early morning; like the flap of a wave; the kiss of a wave; chill and sharp and yet (for a girl of eighteen as she was then) solemn, feeling as she did, standing there at the open window, that something awful was about to happen.

Something awful *will* happen. *Mrs. Dalloway* follows the structure of Shakespearean romance, and, like *The Tempest,* it is driven by the deepest wish: that the dead may be brought back to life. But like Prospero's pageant, Clarissa's party is interrupted by a suddenly unavoidable thought (the suicide of Septimus Smith), and like *The Tempest, Mrs. Dalloway* is driven by the simplest recognition: that everyone will die.

Despite her reputation as a socialite, Clarissa lives with this recognition more intimately than anyone; at Bourton, when she was a child, she saw her sister, Sylvia, crushed by a falling tree. But Clarissa's authority is established not through narrative information but through the quality of her thinking, which the initial movement of the novel's language embodies. The opening eight sentences have the shape and impact of a lyric poem because, like Keats's ode, they deliver us unexpectedly to a thought that seems at odds with the sequence of observations that has also produced it. The knowledge of impending mortality happens to Clarissa, as if for the first time. In the same way, it happens to us.

"The words drop so fast one can't pick them up," said Woolf of her experience of reading Shakespeare. "This is not 'writing' at all. Indeed, I could say that Shakespeare surpasses literature altogether, if I knew what I meant." What Woolf meant, I think, is that reading Shakespeare, she felt inexplicably intimate not with language but with preconscious activity, as if Shakespeare's language were providing unmediated access to the work of the mind, the work she herself aspired to capture in language on the page. To become intimate with Shakespeare is in this sense to become intimate with ourselves, and to do so at the moment when selfhood seems at once most powerful and most tenuous. It is to suffer the beautiful illusion of a fully articulable inner life at the same time that we're offered the terms of articulation—to exist viscerally in the process of change, to relinquish the will to fate.

This is why the great poems of thinking in our language are, like the "Ode to a Nightingale," almost inevitably about what Heidegger called being-towards-death: to become a meditative thinker is to exist not in spite of but because of the fact that one day we will have been.

A full moon. Yesterday, a sheep escaped into the woods,
and not just any sheep—the ram, the whole future.
If we see him again, we'll see his bones.
The grass shudders a little; maybe the wind passed through
    it.
And the new leaves of the olives shudder in the same way.
Mice in the fields. Where the fox hunts,
tomorrow there'll be blood in the grass.
But the storm—the storm will wash it away.

In one window, there's a boy sitting.
He's been sent to bed—too early,
in his opinion. So he sits at the window—

Everything is settled now.
Where you are now is where you'll sleep, where you'll wake
    up in the morning.
The mountain stands like a beacon, to remind the night
    that the earth exists,
that it mustn't be forgotten.

Above the sea, the clouds form as the wind rises,
Dispersing them, giving them a sense of purpose.

Tomorrow the dawn won't come.
The sky won't go back to being the sky of day; it will go
    on as night,
except the stars will fade and vanish as the storm arrives,
lasting perhaps ten hours altogether.
But the world as it was cannot return.

Sentence by sentence, these stanzas from the middle of Louise Glück's "Before the Storm" register their inhabitation of being-towards-death in their very syntax. Tense shifts constantly; the language of temporality is everywhere. "Yesterday, a sheep escaped into the woods," and "tomorrow there'll be blood in the grass," but in no time even this evidence of prior existence will have been: "the storm will wash it away." The ram is "the whole future," but the future persists in this poem only by virtue of our recognition that it will someday be the past.

The choral speaker of "Before the Storm" (a multiplicity of mortal beings speaking as one) is acutely aware of the inexorably forward motion of time, but like Prospero's or Lear's, the speaker's thinking darts in multiple directions at once, as if the poem were a conversation between multiple parties. Every new stanza sounds like the beginning of a new poem—as if to suggest that our experience of the forward motion of time actually inheres in a constant movement back to a beginning, not to the point we first set out from but to a different starting point, one we couldn't have predicted. The poem moves not by projecting a totality out of a single sentence but by evolving (as Coleridge described Shakespearean utterance) B out of A and C out of B: tomorrow the rain will come, yesterday the ram escaped, tonight a boy's been sent to bed early. Quickly we braid these materials into a coherent sense of human mortality, but our incremental experience of the poem is quietly disorienting. For if we pay attention simply to what the poem is saying, the poem says everything is ending. But if we pay attention to how the poem dramatizes its thinking, the poem suggests that we're nonetheless free to re-create our beginning over and over again, turning back from the end. Like Shakespearean romance, the poem grants our deepest wish and at the same time denies it. Like the "Ode to a Nightingale," it denies our deepest wish at the same time that it fulfills us. The ram will die, the boy will grow up, the flock will dwindle, the rain will fall, the dawn won't come, something awful will happen, the world will remain a mystery. "Everything is settled now," says this poem, but the texture of the poem's thinking suggests that nothing is settled. "A turn or two I'll walk," says Prospero, "To still my beating mind," but we know that such turning can only make the mind's beat stronger, which is anyway what we crave.

Such turning has distinguished the manner of some of the most prominent poetry since modernism, allowing us to suffer the misapprehension that disjunctiveness is a characteristic feature of one school of poetry and not another. But the sound of thinking in our poetry has always been disjunctive, and whether we're reading Shakespeare or Keats, Ashbery or Glück, the best image for a poem's ultimate coherence is not the ouroboros, the serpent with its tail in its mouth, but the serpent making a fulcrum of its own body, moving relentlessly yet inexplicably forward. "You seem to be *told* nothing," said Coleridge of the experience of reading Shakespeare, "but to see and hear every thing," and what we hear is "the rapid flow, the quick change, and the playful nature of the thoughts."

Shakespeare was primarily a dramatic poet, but the poetry of his plays has shaped the history of English-language poetry as powerfully as his lyrics, which were themselves shaped by the poetry of drama. Coleridge speculated that Shakespeare developed a purposefully meandering texture in his lyric poems as a way of compensating for the lack of the annotating presence of the actor—the voice and gesture that may transform even the most staid piece of writing into a visceral act of becoming. This seems plausible, except that Shakespeare's dramatic writing also offers this compensation, making his verse feel richly inward on the page and sometimes immune to the missteps of bungling actors.

The verse also keeps us open to missteps. The fact that Shakespeare was not only a poet but also one of the greatest prose writers in the language begs a larger argument, an argument that encompasses not only poetry but also prose; an argument that encompasses not only prose but also the metaphors we employ to represent thinking in most any circumstance; an argument that asks us to see that those metaphors have arisen not from an unmediated encounter with our own thinking but from our devotion to the makers of metaphors; an argument that demands, finally, to be raised to the level of hyperbole. But for Shakespeare, none of us would know what we imagine thinking to be.

All Changed

"The purpose of playing," says Hamlet to the troupe of actors in his play, is "to hold, as 'twere, the mirror up to nature." Yet the most memorable poems are not simply, in the Aristotelian sense, imitations of an action; they are themselves actions, and, finally, the most crucial act of mirroring is the one that takes place between the poems and their readers.

"The greatest poems we will write already exist," I wrote at the beginning of this book, "and the work of a lifetime is to recognize them as our own." To search out excellence in poetry, or anything else, is to join a community, to rely on others for what we do not know, to invite others to rely on us. Yet the poems in which the soul discovers itself at one moment may seem strangely unfamiliar at the next, the mirror gone blank. And the virtues that distinguish one great poem may be utterly lacking in the one we turn to next. Even more threateningly, more beguilingly, those virtues may not be lacking in the next poem but just slightly compromised, our effort to capitalize upon them continually vexed. As we wither in the poems we're given to write, we change—not as we'd like, but as we must.

What happens if we change?

> All changed, changed utterly:
> A terrible beauty is born.

This famous couplet from Yeats's "Easter, 1916" both asserts and obliterates the simplest of all revelations, the one that suddenly interrupts Prospero's pageant, the one that overwhelms Lear on the heath: if we change, we die. The revelation erupts from the poem itself, changing it, because the couplet offers the first enunciation of the simple present tense in the poem: *is*. Everything else has already happened, everyone has changed, but a terrible beauty is born. Recast the second line in past tense, and the magic is lost: "All changed, changed utterly: / A terrible beauty was born." Yeats is speaking about something very large, but the magnitude of his speech depends on something very small.

Strictly speaking, there are three tenses: past, present, and future. But in English each tense may be delivered to us in one of four aspects: simple ("I change"), continuous ("I am changing"), perfect ("I have changed"), and perfect continuous ("I have been changing"). In addition, any combination of tense and aspect may be cast in one of several modes: indicative ("you are changing"), interrogative ("are you changing?"), imperative ("change!"), conditional ("you would be changing"), subjunctive ("if you were changing"), optative ("if only you'd change"). Yeats's poem deploys many of these aspects and modes, but in order to develop a way of thinking about the effect of such rapid variations, I want to begin with a poem in which tense changes much more plainly. The first stanza of John Ashbery's "This Room" contains four sentences, the first three of which are in simple past tense, the last of which is in simple present. The syntax could hardly be more straightforward.

> The room I entered was a dream of this room.
> Surely all those feet on the sofa were mine.
> The oval portrait
> of a dog was me at an early age.
> Something shimmers, something is hushed up.

The first sentence also sets up a relationship between the past ("The room I entered") and the present ("this room"), suggesting that the present moment is an uncanny repetition of a previous moment. In the present moment, something shimmers, but we don't know what it is.

The second and final stanza of "This Room" contains three sentences, the first of which returns to the past tense and features for the first time some dependent syntax. The second sentence shifts again to the present tense, and the shift is not just demanded by the logic of narrative sequence, as a movement from the simple past ("We had macaroni") to the past perfect ("We had had macaroni") might be. Instead, the shift in tense diverts our attention away from a story told about the past to the act of enunciating that story in the present.

> We had macaroni for lunch every day
> except Sunday, when a small quail was induced
> to be served to us. Why do I tell you these things?
> You are not even here.

Many other things might be noticed about this stanza. The second sentence also shifts from the indicative ("We had macaroni") to the interrogative mode ("Why do I tell you?"). And the sentences are distinguished by Ashbery's typically brilliant juxtapositions of Germanic and Latinate diction, from "macaroni for lunch" to "induced / to be served." But the shifts in tense are what drive the poem most forcefully. In the past, feet were placed on the sofa, macaroni was eaten for lunch; this may or may not be interesting. In the present, a story about the past is told but the elements of that story (sofa, oval portrait, macaroni, quail) are long gone, and so is the person to whom the story is told—the person who presumably would care about those elements as deeply as the teller. What might have been a simple (though quirky) narrative about the past becomes a poignant drama enacted in the present, for when the tense shifts, what suddenly matters more than the narrative material as such is the quizzical sense of loss that accrues as we become aware of the act of enunciating the material in the present: "Why do I tell you these things?"

Who are you? The second-person address inevitably invokes the reader, present to his or her own experience of the poem but absent from the poet's experience. But "This Room" is the first poem in *Your Name Here*, a book that bears this dedication: "For Pierre Martory 1920–1998." This you, unlike the reader, was once fully present to the poet, but only in the past. "I saw it with Pierre in the summer of 1959," says Ashbery in one of the narrative moments of "Self-Portrait in a Convex Mirror," recalling the first time he laid eyes on the Parmigianino painting on which his great long poem is so circuitously based. What shimmers in "This Room," what is covered up, is the palpable absence of the dead.

Shifting to the present tense might seem like the inevitable way to throw a poem's weight away from the remembered past to the present dilemma, away from the arena of narrative account to the arena of lyric cry. But before endorsing this generalization, let's consider the operation of tense in a genre that inevitably foregrounds temporality in ways that poems may not: prose fiction. Compare the opening chapter of Defoe's *Robinson Crusoe*—

> I was born in the year 1632, in the city of York, of a good family, though not of that country, my father being a foreigner of Bremen who settled first at Hull. He got a good estate by merchandise and, leaving off his trade, lived afterward at York,

from whence he had married my mother, whose relations were named Robinson, a very good family in that country, and from whom I was called Robinson Kreutznaer; but by the usual corruption of words in England we are now called, nay, we call ourselves, and write our name "Crusoe," and so my companions always called me.

—to the opening chapter of Fitzgerald's *The Great Gatsby*.

In my younger and more vulnerable years my father gave me some advice that I've been turning over in my mind ever since.

"Whenever you feel like criticizing any one," he told me, "just remember that all the people in this world haven't had the advantages that you've had."

He didn't say any more, but we've always been unusually communicative in a reserved way, and I understood that he meant a great deal more than that. In consequence, I'm inclined to reserve all judgments, a habit that has opened up many curious natures to me and also made me the victim of not a few veteran bores. The abnormal mind is quick to detect and attach itself to this quality when it appears in a normal person, and so it came about that in college I was unjustly accused of being a politician, because I was privy to the secret griefs of wild, unknown men.

In the first sentence of *The Great Gatsby* we're immediately asked to pay at least as much attention to the act of narration as to the narrated events. Nick Carraway isn't just telling a story in the simple past ("my father gave me some advice"); he's also thinking in the present perfect continuous ("I've been turning over"). The tense of the first sentence changes dramatically, and by the time we reach the third paragraph, tense is shifting constantly between the past and the present, aspect fluctuating even more rapidly between the simple and the continuous. As a result, we're bound up in the act of narrative enunciation as an event that is happening now. This is why, having read only these five sentences of the novel, we're not surprised when Nick's confession that he's "inclined to reserve all judgments" is immediately compromised by the remark about "veteran bores." He is what we're taught early on to recognize as an unreliable narrator.

Defoe's act of enunciation is also happening now ("I was born in the year 1632"), but in *Robinson Crusoe* we're listening to a narrator who wants to seem at all moments reliable, a purveyor of fact and nothing more. Here, tense does not change. Crusoe tells his story in the simple past ("He got a good estate"), altering the aspect to the past perfect ("he had married my mother") when the temporal logic of events naturally demands that he do so. Those events, more than the act of enunciating them, ask for our attention. But while Defoe was, like other inventors of the novel, intent on giving fiction the sheen of fact, he also delighted in muddying that sheen. The final sentence of his paragraph alerts us to the ways in which even the simplest proper names may be inaccurate, and the novel shifts for the first time to the present tense in order to tell us so ("we are now called") before shifting back to the past ("my companions always called me"). The attentive reader is, after encountering only two sentences of *Robinson Crusoe*, wondering just how factual this account of uncommon adventure is going to be, despite Defoe's assurance in his preface that the book is "a just history of fact; neither is there any appearance of fiction in it."

Defoe and Fitzgerald don't use different means to different ends; what is different is the degree to which similar means are deployed. For in both cases what matters is not the particular direction in which the tense shifts but, first, whether or not tense is shifting at all, and, second, the prominence with which the shifting occurs. Fitzgerald performs these changes flagrantly while Defoe does so more slyly, but both novels harness shifts of tense as a way of drawing our attention toward the act of enunciating the story, thereby raising issues of credibility.

Consider in this light a poem that does the opposite of what Ashbery's "This Room" does, a poem that throws its weight on the act of enunciation by shifting abruptly from present tense to past. These are the first two stanzas of John Donne's "The Indifferent."

> I can love both fair and brown,
> Her whom abundance melts, and her whom want betrays,
> Her who loves loneness best, and her who masks and plays,
>   Her whom the country formed, and whom the town,
>   Her who believes, and her who tries,
>   Her who still weeps with spongy eyes,
>   And her who is dry cork, and never cries;
>   I can love her, and her, and you and you,
>   I can love any, so she be not true.
>
>   Will no other vice content you?
> Will it not serve your turn to do, as did your mothers?
> Or have you all old vices spent, and now would find out
>   others?
>   Or does a fear, that men are true, torment you?
>   Oh we are not, be not you so,
>   Let me, and do you, twenty know.
>   Rob me, but bind me not, and let me go.

> Must I, who came to travail thorough you,
> Grow your fixed subject, because you are true?

Again, there are many other wonderful things to be noticed here, not least Donne's characteristically muscular syntax and visceral epithets ("spongy eyes"). It matters that the first of these nine-line stanzas consists of one sentence with a single independent clause ("I can love") while the second is made of seven sentences, most of them one line long, all but one of them no longer indicative in mood but either interrogative ("Will no other?") or imperative ("Let me") or conditional ("would find"). It also matters that the second stanza shifts, like the penultimate sentence of "This Room," to the intimacy of second-person address.

But whatever has changed over the course of these two stanzas, the present tense has reigned: with the exception of one incursion of the present perfect ("have you all old vices spent") and one instance of futurity that points nonetheless to the present moment ("Will no other vice content you?"), every clause is cast in the simple present. This makes the abrupt change to the simple past, occurring at the onset of the third stanza, feel like the weightiest moment in the poem.

> Venus heard me sigh this song,
> And by love's sweetest part, variety, she swore
> She heard not this till now; and that it should be so no
> more.

Unlike "This Room," "The Indifferent" does not shift our attention from the narration of past material to the present act of enunciation; instead, the poem shifts from the present enunciation of a complaint to the recognition that this enunciation is actually a reenactment of an enunciation that took place in the past: "Venus heard me sigh this song." But the tense shift in Donne's poem nonetheless bears the same kind of weight: it asks us to focus our attention less on what the poem says than on the dramatic act of saying it. The distinction here is not so cleanly between narrative material ("We had macaroni") and lyric cry ("Why do I tell you?"), but the shift in tense similarly forces us to sharpen our relationship to the poem as a dramatic utterance, an event that happens as we hear it. By the end of the poem, the "you" who dominates the second stanza has become ancillary to the poem's most potent drama, which takes place between the poet and the goddess of love. This is why Donne's poem feels as brilliantly cold as Ashbery's does intimate.

The temptation to generalize at this point is acute. Some poems, like the ones I've examined so far, shift overtly and decisively from one tense to another. Other poems shift constantly. But tense is one tool among others, and there are many great lyric poems in which tense never changes at all. The simple present has been for centuries the signature tense of the lyric, which is why lyric poems so often possess a dreamlike intensity of vision; as Freud points out, dreams transform the optative mood of our wishes ("if only you were alive") to the simple present ("you are alive!"). But poems that never stray from this tense must throw their weight on the act of enunciation by other means, often by foregrounding syntactical repetition (think of Whitman), by capitalizing on elaborate patterns of sound (think of Keats), or by reducing the prominence of narrative information (think of Dickinson). Increasingly, writers of the American short story have borrowed the quick-fix immediacy of the lyric present, and, like writers of the run-of-the-mill American free-verse poem, they risk staleness to the degree that other ways of provoking our interest in the act of enunciation have not been deployed.

Consider the final paragraphs of *Mrs. Dalloway*: here, the

party toward which the entire novel has pointed is ending; the most prominent characters involved are Richard and Clarissa Dalloway, their daughter, Elizabeth, and Clarissa's old friends Sally Seaton and Peter Walsh.

> For her father [Richard Dalloway] had been look-
> ing at her, as he stood talking to the Bradshaws, and
> he had thought to himself, Who is that lovely girl?
> And suddenly he realized that it was his Elizabeth,
> and he had not recognized her, she looked so lovely
> in her pink frock! Elizabeth had felt him looking at
> her as she talked to Willie Titcomb. So she went
> to him and they stood together, now that the party
> was almost over, looking at the people going, and
> the rooms getting emptier and emptier, with things
> scattered on the floor. Even Ellie Henderson was
> going, nearly last of all, though no one had spoken
> to her, but she had wanted to see everything, to tell
> Edith. And Richard and Elizabeth were rather glad
> it was over, but Richard was proud of his daugh-
> ter. And he had not meant to tell her, but he could
> not help telling her. He had looked at her, he said,
> and he had wondered, Who is that lovely girl? and
> it was his daughter! That did make her happy. But
> her poor dog was howling.
>
> "Richard has improved. You are right," said Sally.
> "I shall go and talk to him. I shall say good-night.
> What does the brain matter," said Lady Rosseter,
> getting up, "compared with the heart?"
>
> "I will come," said Peter, but he sat on for a mo-
> ment. What is this terror? what is this ecstasy? he

thought to himself. What is it that fills me with
extraordinary excitement?

It is Clarissa, he said.

For there she was.

Woolf's deployment of tenses in this passage is at once simple
and complex. Simple, because every change in tense is demanded
by the straightforward logic of narrative temporality. The action
is presented in the past tense ("he realized"), necessitating in-
cursions into the past perfect ("he had thought") and the past
perfect continuous ("he had been looking") to describe earlier
actions. The present tense is logically deployed when conversation is recounted ("You are right"), the future tense when conversation alludes to events about to happen ("I shall go and talk
to him"). By the same logic, the present tense is also deployed
when the unspoken thoughts of the characters are recounted
("What is this terror?").

But something more magical than logical seems nonetheless
to be happening when the tense shifts from present to past in
the final two sentences of *Mrs. Dalloway*.

It is Clarissa, he said.

For there she was.

This recognition of Clarissa Dalloway by Peter Walsh echoes
the earlier, less momentous recognition of Elizabeth Dalloway
by her father, Richard, the tense shifting placidly from "is" to
"was"—

Who is that lovely girl? And suddenly he realized
that it was his Elizabeth.

—but at the end of the book the shift from the present tense of
recounted thought ("It is Clarissa") to the narrative's governing

past tense ("For there she was") is stripped of the trappings of discursiveness ("And suddenly he realized"), allowing the shift to feel unhinged from the logic of temporality, rather than demanded by it. For a second, Clarissa both is and was—she exists simultaneously in the past and the present, as if she were both alive and dead, a ghost of herself, an ecstasy. Her party is both a resurrection of the dead and a reminder that everyone will die, and when Clarissa herself reappears in the novel's final sentences, she is simultaneously reborn ("It is Clarissa") and remanded back into the custody of the doomed ("there she was"). Cast Woolf's novel in the present tense—"It is Clarissa, he says. For there she is"—and the magic is lost.

In a brief essay called "Fear of Breakdown," D. W. Winnicott wonders why people so often fear something that has already happened, as if the past were an impending future. He concludes that the present is an oddly difficult place to live. Events, especially traumatic events, will not recede into the past if they have not fully been experienced in the present moment of their happening; in order to remember the event, to put it once and for all into the past, the event needs to happen again. For Winnicott, the relationship between analyst and patient creates the space where this transaction occurs, but something like it also occurs in the language of the lyric, to which the conclusion of *Mrs. Dalloway* aspires. The past is pulled into the present so that it might recede definitively into the past, threatening no longer to be traumatic. "Why do I tell you these things?" asks Ashbery, shifting to the present tense to address a dead person as a living person. "You are not even here," he then says, letting that person fall back into oblivion.

"Easter, 1916," Yeats's great poem about the Easter Rebellion, the quickly aborted declaration of an Irish republic, enacts this dialogue with the dead on a grander scale. The poem looks back on events that have happened, at the revolutionaries who were executed by the British government; but the poem longs for the present tense. The third of its four stanzas (the only stanza not containing the famous refrain "a terrible beauty is born") exists exclusively in the simple present tense of the lyric moment.

> Hearts with one purpose alone
> Through summer and winter seem
> Enchanted to a stone
> To trouble the living stream.
> The horse that comes from the road,
> The rider, the birds that range
> From cloud to tumbling cloud,
> Minute by minute they change;
> A shadow of cloud on the stream
> Changes minute by minute;
> A horse-hoof slides on the brim,
> And a horse plashes within it;
> The long-legged moor-hens dive,
> And hens to moor-cocks call;
> Minute by minute they live:
> The stone's in the midst of all.

Reiterated so determinedly, the simple present tense produces a timeless presence. Everything surrounding the stone may be changing, but this state of constant mutability feels mythic, always happening, always having happened: things variously *seem, come, range, change, slide, plash, dive, call,* and *live.* This is the present tense to which the entire poem aspires in its other three stanzas.

Until the first instance of the refrain, the opening stanza's dominant tense is the present perfect: *I have met, I have passed, I have lingered, I have said, I have thought.* What we have here so far, once again, is a narrative—a story about people who once seemed ordinary but who unexpectedly turn out to be astonishing.

> I have met them at close of day
> Coming with vivid faces
> From counter or desk among grey
> Eighteenth-century houses.
> I have passed with a nod of the head
> Or polite meaningless words,
> Or have lingered awhile and said
> Polite meaningless words,
> And thought before I had done
> Of a mocking tale or a gibe
> To please a companion
> Around the fire at the club,
> Being certain that they and I
> But lived where motley is worn:
> All changed, changed utterly:
> A terrible beauty is born.

The grammar of the penultimate line ("All changed") is strategically ambiguous; *change* could be a simple past tense verb (*they all changed*) or a predicate adjective (*all are changed*). But because of the repetition of the present perfect in the independent clauses of the previous sentences, we're most likely to read the penultimate line as one more iteration of that tense: *all have changed*. Then, with the shift to the simple present in the final line, everything changes. As in the poems I've examined by Ashbery and Donne, the change in tense suddenly throws a great deal of weight on the act of enunciation: the poem is looking at events that occurred in the past, but something is happening right now, in the time it takes to speak the words of the poem.

The second stanza of "Easter, 1916" follows a similar pattern:

it tells stories about the various revolutionaries, employing the past, past perfect, and present perfect tenses before shifting to the simple present in the final line. But in this stanza, one earlier present-tense line ("Yet I number him in the song") prepares us for that shift.

> This other man I had dreamed
> A drunken, vainglorious lout.
> He had done most bitter wrong
> To some who are near my heart,
> Yet I number him in the song;
> He, too, has resigned his part
> In the casual comedy;
> He, too, has been changed in his turn,
> Transformed utterly:
> A terrible beauty is born.

Here, the grammar of the penultimate line is no longer ambiguous: Yeats employs the present perfect (*he has been changed, transformed utterly*) and, once again, the final line's shift to the simple present diverts attention from the stories told to the act of telling. More specifically, Yeats diverts our attention from John MacBride, the executed revolutionary who had married Yeats's beloved Maud Gonne, to the act of singing about MacBride in the present. What is the logic here? If the phrase *all have changed* becomes *all have been changed*, who is doing the changing? Is a terrible beauty born because something momentous happened in the past or because Yeats numbers this man in his song in the present?

Following on the richly lyrical third stanza about the stone in the midst of the changing stream, the fourth and final stanza clarifies this logic, lifting the entire act of the poem into the present tense.

And what if excess of love
Bewildered them till they died?
I write it out in a verse—
MacDonagh and MacBride
And Connolly and Pearse
Now and in time to be,
Wherever green is worn,
Are changed, changed utterly:
A terrible beauty is born.

A great many things are happening simultaneously here. Yeats is admitting that the previously unnamed revolutionaries may have acted carelessly, without regard for their own lives, know-ing the rebellion was doomed. At the same time, he fits their surnames seamlessly into the poem's long sequence of iambic trimeter lines, making the recitation of those names feel (for all their historical specificity) oracular, a lyric flight driven by a relentless rhythmic intensity. Most potently, Yeats shifts to the present tense not in the last line but in the sixth-to-last line, ask-ing us to see the extraordinary transformation that has occurred not as the result of events as such but as the result of a way of thinking and feeling about those events in the present: "I write it out in a verse." The penultimate line, which in the first and second stanzas remained lodged in the present perfect, is now iterated confidently in the present: *all are changed*. The revolu-tionaries are pulled into the lyric moment, and they change now and forever, just as (in the third stanza) a cloud on the stream changes or a horse plashes or a moor-hen dives.

It's not enough to enact this transformation once. This is why refrain is so crucial to Yeats's poem: "A terrible beauty is born." The line must be said again, and then again, the past dragged into the present so that the trauma of the Easter Rebellion, difficult to process at the historical moment of its happening, might truly be experienced. It is not possible to remember what has not yet happened, and by driving into the present, "Easter, 1916" gives us the gift of the past, allowing change to mean for a moment something other than death, allowing death to become something other than annihilation.

I think this feeling of transformation, of an action taking place in real time, the time it takes to read the poem, is what we crave from poetry, even if a poem spends most of its energy recounting an event that has already happened. To crave change is to court mortality, the event toward which all change points, but poems afford us the opportunity to experience loss as gain, absence as presence: our experience of the language fulfills us even as we're asked to inhabit the future perfect—the knowledge that one day we will have been. "This Room" enacts this paradoxical transaction with great economy, its shift to the present tense both conjuring and burying the dead: "Why do I tell you these things?"

No two poems ask us to change in exactly the same way, but the greater wonder is that, like all works of art, poems produce such rich and complicated effects with such extraordinarily limited means. Big words and small words. Stressed and unstressed syllables. The past tense and the present. What's more, the effects are infinitely repeatable, a beauty born each time we take the journey from the first word of a poem to the last.

Every human being participates in life-changing events and suffers powerful feelings; poems are forged from the shared medium of our language. But language does not inevitably become a poem—a verbal artifact that makes patterns from the medium's limited means, asking us to live as viscerally in the relationship of stressed and unstressed syllables as we imagine we live in our minds. The origins of any particular poem are mysterious, perhaps more mysterious than the origins of words themselves, but the virtues of poetry exist as the material fact of language on the page, and, in this sense, the future of poetry is right before our eyes. We finish the poem, we finish the book, we put it down, we are changed.

That was wonderful, we say. For here it is.

Acknowledgments

During the many years that I've been writing this book, pieces of its chapters have appeared in different forms in the *Antioch Review, Boston Review, The Cambridge Companion to English Poets, Conjunctions,* the *Kenyon Review, Literary Imagination,* the *Nation, New England Review, The Oxford Handbook of Shakespeare's Poetry, Poetry Northwest, Raritan, Salmagundi, Southwest Review, Virginia Quarterly Review, Walt Whitman: Where the Future Becomes Present,* and the *Yale Review,* and I am deeply grateful to the editors who supported and in many cases inspired my thinking.

Jeremy Bass, Kenneth Gross, and Ellen Bryant Voigt read the manuscript as it grew. Joanna Scott did that and more, since it was our daily conversation about the life of writing that prompted these sentences and, over time, allowed them to cohere.

Bibliography

Ashbery, John. *Chinese Whispers*. New York: Farrar, Straus and Giroux, 2002.

———. *Collected Poems, 1956–1987*. Edited by Mark Ford. New York: Library of America, 2008.

———. *Girls on the Run*. New York: Farrar, Straus and Giroux, 1999.

———. *Selected Prose*. Edited by Eugene Richie. Ann Arbor: University of Michigan Press, 2004.

———. *Where Shall I Wander*. New York: Ecco Press, 2005.

———. *Your Name Here*. New York: Farrar, Straus and Giroux, 2000.

Auden, W. H. "Yeats as an Example." *Kenyon Review* 10 (1948): 187–95.

Barthes, Roland. *S/Z*. Translated by Richard Miller. New York: Farrar, Straus and Giroux, 1974.

Bishop, Elizabeth. *Poems, Prose, and Letters*. Edited by Robert Giroux and Lloyd Schwartz. New York: Library of America, 2008.

———. *Words in Air: The Complete Correspondence between Elizabeth Bishop and Robert Lowell*. Edited by Thomas Travisano with Saskia Hamilton. New York: Farrar, Straus and Giroux, 2008.

Blake, William. *The Complete Poetry and Prose*. Edited by David V. Erdman. New York: Anchor Books, 1988.

Coleridge, Samuel Taylor. *Biographia Literaria*. Edited by James Engell and W. Jackson Bate. Princeton. NJ: Princeton University Press, 1983.

———. *Table Talk*. In *The Romantics on Shakespeare*, edited by Jonathan Bate, 160–63. New York: Penguin, 1992.

Defoe, Daniel. *Robinson Crusoe*. Edited by Harvey Swados. New York: New American Library, 1980.

Dickinson, Emily. *The Letters*. Edited by Thomas H. Johnson and Theodora Ward. 3 vols. Cambridge, MA: Harvard University Press, 1958.

———. *The Poems: Variorum Edition*. Edited by R. W. Franklin. 3 vols. Cambridge, MA: Harvard University Press, 1998.

Donne, John. *The Major Works*. Edited by John Carey. New York: Oxford University Press, 1990.

Eliot, T. S. *The Complete Poems and Plays*. New York: Harcourt, 1971.

Fitzgerald, F. Scott. *The Great Gatsby*. New York: Charles Scribner's Sons, 1925.

Freud, Sigmund. *The Interpretation of Dreams*. Translated by James Strachey. New York: Avon Books, 1965.

Giles, Herbert. *A History of Chinese Literature*. New York: Appleton, 1901.

Glück, Louise. *Averno*. New York: Farrar, Straus and Giroux, 2006.

———. *A Village Life*. New York: Farrar, Straus and Giroux, 2009.

Gordon, Lyndall. *Lives Like Loaded Guns: Emily Dickinson and Her Family's Feuds*. New York: Viking, 2010.

Heidegger, Martin. *Being and Time*. Translated by John Macquarrie and Edward Robinson. New York: Harper and Row, 1962.

———. *Discourse on Thinking*. Translated by John M. Anderson and E. Hans Freund. New York: Harper and Row, 1966.

Herbert, George. *The English Poems*. Edited by C. A. Patrides. London: J. M. Dent, 1974.

Howe, Susan. *The Nonconformist's Manual*. New York: New Directions, 1993.

James, William. *Pragmatism and The Meaning of Truth*. Cambridge, MA: Harvard University Press, 1978.

Jarrell, Randall. *The Complete Poems*. New York: Farrar, Straus and Giroux, 1969.

———. *Poetry and the Age*. New York: Vintage, 1953.

Keats, John. *The Letters*. Edited by Hyder Edward Rollins. 2 vols. Cambridge, MA: Harvard University Press, 1958.

————. *The Poems*. Edited by Jack Stillinger. London: Heinemann, 1978.

Levinas, Emmanuel. *Of God Who Comes to Mind*. Translated by Bettina Bergo. Stanford, CA: Stanford University Press, 1998.

————. *Totality and Infinity*. Translated by Alphonso Lingis. Pittsburgh: Duquense University Press, 1961.

Lowell, Robert. *Collected Poems*. Edited by Frank Bidart and David Gewanter with DeSales Harrison. New York: Farrar, Straus and Giroux, 2003.

————. *Collected Prose*. Edited by Robert Giroux. New York: Farrar, Straus and Giroux, 1987.

————. *Words in Air: The Complete Correspondence between Elizabeth Bishop and Robert Lowell*. Edited by Thomas Travisano with Saskia Hamilton. New York: Farrar, Straus and Giroux, 2008.

MacNeice, Louis. *The Poetry of W. B. Yeats*. London: Faber and Faber, 1967.

Marvell, Andrew. *The Complete Poems*. Edited by E. S. Donno. New York: Penguin, 1976.

Oppen, George. *New Collected Poems*. Edited by Michael Davidson. New York: New Directions, 2002.

Phillips, Adam. *On Balance*. London: Hamish Hamilton, 2010.

Pound, Ezra. *Literary Essays*. Edited by T. S. Eliot. New York: New Directions, 1968.

————. *Personae*. Edited by Lea Baechler and A. Walton Litz. New York: New Directions, 1990.

————. *The Pisan Cantos*. Edited by Richard Sieburth. New York: New Directions, 2003.

Proust, Marcel. *Within a Budding Grove*. Translated by C. K. Scott Moncrieff and Terence Kilmartin, revised by D. J. Enright. New York: Modern Library, 1992.

Rich, Adrienne. *On Lies, Secrets, and Silence*. New York: Norton, 1979.

Saddlemyer, Anne. *Becoming George: The Life of Mrs. W. B. Yeats*. New York: Oxford University Press, 2002.

Shakespeare, William. *The Complete Works: The New Pelican Text.* Edited by Stephen Orgel and A. R. Braunmuller. New York: Penguin, 2002.

Stevens, Wallace. *Collected Poetry and Prose.* Edited by Frank Kermode and Joan Richardson. New York: Library of America, 1997.

———. *Letters.* Edited by Holly Stevens. New York: Knopf, 1966.

Tennyson, Alfred. *The Poems.* Edited by Christopher Ricks. London: Longmans, 1969.

Voigt, Ellen Bryant. "Double Talk and Double Vision." *Michigan Quarterly Review* 48 (2009): 373–85.

Whitman, Walt. *Complete Poetry and Collected Prose.* Edited by Justin Kaplan. New York: Library of America, 1982.

Winnicott, D. W. *The Child, the Family, and the Outside World.* New York: Perseus, 1987.

———. *Psycho-Analytic Explorations.* Edited by Clare Winnicott, Ray Shepherd, and Madeleine Davis. Cambridge, MA: Harvard University Press, 1989.

Woolf, Virginia. *Mrs. Dalloway.* New York: Harcourt, 1925.

———. *A Writer's Diary.* Edited by Leonard Woolf. London: Hogarth Press, 1953.

Yeats, George, and Yeats, W. B. *The Letters.* Edited by Anne Saddlemyer. New York: Oxford University Press, 2011.

Yeats, W. B. *Early Essays.* Edited by Richard Finneran and George Bornstein. New York: Scribner, 2007.

———. *The Poems.* Edited by Richard Finneran. New York: Macmillan, 1989.

———. *A Vision.* New York: Macmillan, 1956.

———. *Yeats's Vision Papers.* Edited by George Mills Harper, assisted by Mary Jane Harper. 3 vols. Iowa City: University of Iowa Press, 1992.

Index

Antonioni, Michelangelo, 42, 43, 45, 47

"Armadillo, The" (Bishop), 108

Ashbery, John, 104, 113–23, 142–44, 147, 149, 152, 154, 157

"As I Ebb'd with the Ocean of Life" (Whitman), 68–75

Auden, W. H., 21, 25, 96

Avventura, L' (Antonioni), 42, 43, 45, 47

Barthes, Roland, 48

Baudelaire, Charles, 5, 80

Beethoven, Ludwig van, 42, 43, 45, 47, 50

"Before the Storm" (Glück), 137–39

"Bight, The" (Bishop), 105–6

Bishop, Elizabeth, 41–42, 43, 50–53, 103–11, 115

Blake, William, 5, 8–10, 11, 22, 77–79, 81, 83, 87–89, 91

"Brazil, January 1, 1502" (Bishop), 41–42, 43, 50–53

Byron, George Gordon, 7

Cantos, The (Pound), 30, 34, 37, 97. See also *Pisan Cantos, The*

Chants Democratic and Native American (Whitman), 74

Chinese Whispers (Ashbery), 117–18

"Choice, The" (Yeats), 18–19

Coleridge, Samuel Taylor, 128, 132, 139, 140

"Coma Berenices" (Ashbery), 118–19

"Coming of Wisdom with Time, The" (Yeats), 3

"Coole and Ballylee, 1931" (Yeats), 6–7, 10

Coriolanus (Shakespeare), 53–54

"Crossing Brooklyn Ferry" (Whitman), 74

"Death of a Soldier, The" (Stevens), 96–98, 99

Defoe, Daniel, 144–45, 146–47

"Dialogue of Self and Soul, A" (Yeats), 19, 21

Dickinson, Austin, 55–57

Dickinson, Emily, 55–63, 65, 67–68, 70, 83–84, 86, 89, 100, 101, 123, 149

Dickinson, Lavinia ("Vinnie"), 57

Dickinson, Susan Gilbert, 55–57, 59

Discrete Series (Oppen), 14

Dolphin, The (Lowell), 109

Don Juan (Byron), 7

Donne, John, 147–49, 154

Draft of XVI Cantos, A (Pound), 97

"Dry Salvages, The" (Eliot), 44–48, 50, 52

"East Coker" (Eliot), 46, 47

"Easter, 1916" (Yeats), 141–42, 152–57

Eliot, T. S., 28, 34–39, 44–48, 50, 52, 81, 92, 101, 110, 113, 119–20

"Esthétique du Mal" (Stevens), 98–99

"Eve of St. Agnes, The" (Keats), 43, 44

"Fan-Piece, for Her Imperial Lord" (Pound), 27–30, 33, 36, 75

"Father's Bedroom" (Lowell), 108–9

"Fish, The" (Yeats), 4–6, 8

Fitzgerald, F. Scott, 145–47

Four Quartets (Eliot), 44–48, 50, 52, 81

"French Revolution, The" (Blake), 87–89

Freud, Sigmund, 29, 132, 149

"Garden, The" (Marvell), 9, 10–12

Giles, Herbert, 27–29, 39

Girls on the Run (Ashbery), 120–21

Glück, Louise, 66–67, 68, 70, 72, 74–75, 137–40

Gonne, Iseult, 17, 18, 20

Gonne, Maud, 17, 155

Great Gatsby, The (Fitzgerald), 145–47

Gunn, Thom, 8

Hamlet (Shakespeare), 49, 141

Hardwick, Elizabeth, 109

Harmonium (Stevens), 93, 97, 98

Heidegger, Martin, 130, 137

Henry the Sixth (Shakespeare), 126–28, 134

Herbert, George, 14

"Hölderlin Marginalia" (Ashbery), 115–16

Howe, Susan, 37–39

"I cannot live with You" (Dickinson), 60–62, 65, 67–68

"Idea of Order at Key West, The" (Stevens), 93

"I felt a Cleaving in my Mind" (Dickinson), 62

"In a Station of the Metro" (Pound), 29, 30

"Indifferent, The" (Donne), 147–49

"Inlet" (Oppen), 12–14

In Memoriam (Tennyson), 30, 33–34, 39–40

In Search of Lost Time (Proust), 3, 12, 14, 15

"Insurance and Social Change" (Stevens), 92

"In the Village" (Bishop), 109–10

"Irrational Element in Poetry, The" (Stevens), 95, 98

James, William, 21
Jarrell, Randall, 103, 104, 114, 115, 116, 119
Jerusalem (Blake), 75, 87
Jonson, Ben, 8
"Jordan I" (Herbert), 14

Keats, John, 43, 44, 84, 86, 89, 132–34, 136, 137, 139, 140, 149
King Lear (Shakespeare), 41, 43, 48–50, 55, 128–31, 132, 142

"Lake Isle of Innisfree, The" (Yeats), 95–96, 99
Leaves of Grass (Whitman), 30, 33, 65, 74, 75
Lemercier, Eugène, 97
"Lettres d'un Soldat" (Stevens), 97
Levinas, Emmanuel, 67–68, 70
Life Studies (Lowell), 101–3, 108, 109, 110
"Lightning Conductor, The" (Ashbery), 117–18
"Lines written a few miles above Tintern Abbey" (Wordsworth), 132
Lord Weary's Castle (Lowell), 102, 104, 105, 110
"Love Song of J. Alfred Prufrock, The" (Eliot), 119–20
Lowell, Robert, 95, 101–11, 113, 123

Macbeth (Shakespeare), 49
MacBride, John, 155, 156
MacNeice, Louis, 96, 99
"Man and the Echo" (Yeats), 25–26
"Marriage of Heaven and Hell, The" (Blake), 79
Marvell, Andrew, 9, 10–12, 14, 15, 94
Materials, The (Oppen), 14
"Men That Are Falling, The" (Stevens), 91–92, 94, 95
Michael Robartes and the Dancer (Yeats), 22–25
Milton (Blake), 87
Milton, John, 132
Moore, Marianne, 25, 92
"Moving" (Jarrell), 114–15
Mrs. Dalloway (Woolf), 135–37, 149–52

North & South (Bishop), 104, 105

"Ode to a Nightingale" (Keats), 133–34, 137, 139
O'Hara, Frank, 113–14
"On Sitting Down to Read *King Lear* Once Again" (Keats), 132–33
Oppen, George, 12–15
Othello (Shakespeare), 43

Phillips, Adam, 77
Pisan Cantos, The (Pound), 6, 75, 77, 80–83, 84–86, 87, 88–89
Poems Written in Discouragement (Yeats), 22

"Postcard from the Volcano, A"
(Stevens), 92
Pound, Ezra, 6, 17, 27–33, 36–37,
38, 44, 45, 77, 80–86, 87,
88–89, 91
"Prayer for My Daughter, A"
(Yeats), 22–23, 25
Prelude, The (Wordsworth), 30
Proust, Marcel, 3, 12, 14, 15

Ransom, John Crowe, 119
Responsibilities (Yeats), 21–22
Rich, Adrienne, 102
"River of Rivers in Connecticut,
The" (Stevens), 92, 93–94, 97
Robinson Crusoe (Defoe), 144–45,
146–47
Rosenthal, M. L., 108

Santayana, George, 104
"Second Coming, The" (Yeats), 22,
23–25
"Self-Portrait in a Convex Mirror"
(Ashbery), 144
Shakespeare, William, 5, 36, 41,
43, 48–50, 53–54, 56, 125–40,
141, 142
"Sick Rose, The" (Blake), 8–10, 75,
77–79, 81, 83, 88
"Silence Wager Stories" (Howe),
37–39
Simpson, Louis, 113–14
"Skunk Hour" (Lowell), 108–9
"Snow Man, The" (Stevens), 92, 97
"Song of Myself" (Whitman), 74, 80
"Songs for a Colored Singer"
(Bishop), 104

"Soonest Mended" (Ashbery),
116–17
"Soul selects her own Society, The"
(Dickinson), 63
Stevens, Wallace, 91–100, 114,
132
"Sunday Morning" (Stevens), 132
"Surety and Fidelity Claims"
(Stevens), 93

"Telescope" (Glück), 66–67, 68, 70,
72, 74–75
Tempest, The (Shakespeare), 36,
125–26, 131, 136, 142
Tennyson, Alfred, 30, 33–34,
39–40
"This Room" (Ashbery), 142–44,
147, 148, 152, 157
"To Be Carved on a Stone at Thoor
Ballylee" (Yeats), 26
Todd, Mabel Loomis, 55–57, 59,
62, 63
"Tower, The" (Yeats), 8
Tristan und Isolde (Wagner), 35, 37,
38, 39

"Vastest earthly Day, The"
(Dickinson), 83–84, 86
"Villanelle: The Psychological
Hour" (Pound), 30–33, 36,
38, 85
Vision, A (Yeats), 20, 21
Voigt, Ellen Bryant, 123

Wagner, Richard, 35, 37, 39
"Waking Early Sunday Morning"
(Lowell), 101, 102

Waste Land, The (Eliot), 34–37, 38–39, 44, 45, 46, 50, 97

"Water" (Lowell), 111

"When I have fears that I may cease to be" (Keats), 84

"When I Heard the Learn'd Astronomer" (Whitman), 65–66, 70

Where Shall I Wander (Ashbery), 118–19, 120, 121–23

"Where Shall I Wander" (Ashbery), 121–23

"Where the Rainbow Ends" (Lowell), 102

Whitman, Walt, 30, 33, 65–66, 68–75, 80, 81, 91, 100, 149

"Wild Swans at Coole, The" (Yeats), 6, 7–8, 9

Williams, William Carlos, 92

Winding Stair, The (Yeats), 19

Winnicott, D. W., 121, 152

Winters, Yvor, 8

Woolf, Virginia, 135–37, 149–52

Wordsworth, William, 132

Wright, James, 48

Yeats, Anne, 21, 23

Yeats, George, 17–22, 26

Yeats, W. B., 3, 4–10, 17–26, 27, 74, 94, 95–96, 99, 101, 141–42, 152–57

Your Name Here (Ashbery), 144

James Longenbach is the author of four poetry collections, including *The Iron Key* and *Draft of a Letter*, and six works of criticism, including *The Art of the Poetic Line* and *The Resistance to Poetry*, as well as numerous essays and reviews. He is Joseph Henry Gilmore Professor of English at the University of Rochester.

Book design by Connie Kuhnz. Composition by BookMobile Design and Digital Publisher Services, Minneapolis, Minnesota. Manufactured by Versa Press on acid-free 30 percent post-consumer wastepaper.